Between Worlds
Essays on Culture and Belonging

Marilyn R. Gardner
Illustrations by Annie Rebekah Gardner

Doorlight Publications
www.doorlightpubs.com

Text copyright ©2014 Marilyn R. Gardner
Illustrations copyright ©2014 Annie Rebekah Gardner
Cover Photo, Hagia Sophia, copyright ©2014 Carol Brown

First published 2014 by Doorlight Publications.

ISBN 0-9838653-8-8
ISBN13 978-0-9838653-8-4

Design & Production by Ruth Anne Burke

To my children,
Annie, Joel, Micah, Stefanie, Jonathan
who know well what it is to live between
worlds.

To my parents who loved me well
through a childhood spent in Pakistan and
the United States.

Most of all to my husband Cliff,
who has traveled between worlds by
my side for many years and continually
encourages me to write about it.

Contents

Preface

I was born on a furlough when my parents were enjoying a well-needed break in their home country. I was not born in a tired mission hospital, surrounded by white-clad nurses and well-scrubbed doctors who were rejoicing in the birth of "one of their own." Instead I was born in a small town in Massachusetts known for its wooden toys, symbolized by a large wooden rocking horse for all to see in the center of town.

I don't like that I was born in America. It hurts my pride, my well-crafted sense of being other. But I was, and that is part of my story.

Arriving as a girl in an already well-established family of boys gave me special privilege. I was born into princess status and knew it well. When I was three-months old I was packed up with my dollies and my diapers, to embark on the 6-week journey it would take my family to get from the shores of New

York City to the chaos of Karachi Harbor. At four months Pakistan became part of the fabric of my life, weaving its way into my heart and soul. This book is a product of that life, a life lived on both sides of the globe. It is a set of essays from a life lived between worlds.

The book began with a blog started in 2011 called *Communicating Across Boundaries* and I owe much to my readers, who read, commented, encouraged and emailed. I could not have written this without the encouragement they unknowingly gave. I am grateful to my daughter Annie for the beautiful pen and ink illustrations that she crafted for *Between Worlds*. I also want to thank my editorial team – my editor extraordinaire, Daniel Brown, who made the process of crafting and recrafting words something to enjoy and not dread.

It is my hope that my words, stories, thoughts, and feelings resonate with those who, along with me, are living between worlds.

—Cambridge, Massachusetts
May, 2014

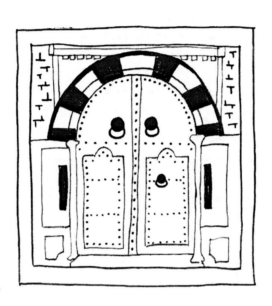

Home

In the hall of an old Inn by the ocean is a sign that reads 'Home is Where Our Story Begins.' But if home is where our story begins, what happens when we can't go back?

Where My Story Begins

The call to prayer awoke us at the first light of dawn. It was hauntingly melodic and loud. Although it was not yet summer, we felt the heat of Sindh even in those early morning hours. To keep cool we slept on rope beds, *charpais*, set on the flat roof and shrouded with mosquito netting, our gauzy protection against the insects known to bring about the raging fevers of malaria.

This is my earliest memory. I was four years old. A faded black and white photograph confirms the image. Smiling beneath the white netting, I look at the camera while my older brother Tommy, sitting on his bed beside mine, looks at me. In the growing light and amidst the sounds from the mosque down the street, we tried to keep quiet as long as we could but it was a losing battle. Our mother's pleading that we try to get more sleep was met with muffled voices and eyes wide with the wonder of morning. Finally she would give in and allow us to fully wake, joining our voices with the roosters, the birds, and the *Muezzin*.

We lived in a large house with 30-foot ceilings in the heart of Ratodero, a small city in the Sindh region of Pakistan. We were the only foreigners in the city and we had the only car.

Our house, where Bibles abounded and daily prayer was our sustenance, was surrounded on four sides by mosques. The call to prayer did not only wake us in the morning; it was our melody at lunch, our call to afternoon tea, and our mournful melancholy in the evening hours.

Three courtyards at three different levels gave us outdoor space to play and high walls surrounded the entire house. A trough that had at one time been used to water animals became our swimming pool in the hot months and we lived quiet noisy lives in this place. Other homes contribute far more memories to this narrative, but this house shaped me in ways I will never know. Stucco-colored rusty brown, it had arched doors and concrete floors. It was beautiful. It was in this house that I spent time with dolls and brothers, my earliest play mates; this house where I would sleep under billowy mosquito netting cuddled up with my thumb in my mouth; this house that captures a portion of my memory. This house was the beginning.

In the hall of an old Inn by the ocean is a sign that reads *"Home is Where Our Story Begins."* For a third culture kid who questions the definition of home, this is both reassuring and sad. If home is where our story begins, what happens when we cannot go back?

The word 'story' is the key. Third culture kids have stories. Their stories are detailed and vibrant. Stories of travel between worlds, of cross cultural relationships and connections, of grief and of loss, of goodbyes and hellos and more goodbyes.

In Exodus God repeatedly tells the people of Israel to remember their story, to remember their beginning, to remember who they are. Later, exiled in Babylon, unable to return home, they were to remember their stories - stories of wonder and deliverance, of the power of God and His provision. They were to remember their beginnings.

And so I begin by going back to the beginning, to those first memories of which I am never quite certain. Was it my memory? Or was the image planted in my mind by a photograph or a story? I don't know. But I do know that this is where my story begins. This is Home.

Home

I have done a lot of thinking through the years about home. The dictionary definition does not satisfy me, despite more than eleven entries labeled *n.* and various others labeled *adv.* and *adj.*

What is home? When you have moved constantly, you ask yourself that question often. Those of us who work with displaced people, the homeless, or refugees, ask ourselves even more often. Mom taught me early in life that *"Home is where your suitcase is."* I don't know if it is an original "Polly" quote, but it certainly became a theme for us. As I grew older the quote grew in meaning. Perhaps mom was passing this on to her children as a way of reconciling the huge gulf of oceans and cultures separating the home in Massachusetts where she was raised, and her life in Pakistan. Her words became more and more poignant as I grew older and left Pakistan for the United States. When I began to realize that I was responsible for creating home, her words, by this time deeply ingrained in me, were a valuable tool. I was the one in charge of passing on wisdom, starting traditions, planting roots where there seemed to be rootlessness, providing all the textures, sounds, and smells that make up home.

Many of us have a visceral response to places that remind us of home. Places sometimes evoke a childhood that was secure and filled with light. Sometimes smells and sounds suddenly transport us to a place and time that represents home. The smell of sugar cookies baking in an oven or chicken curry cooking on the stove can make us long for a place we can barely remember. Similarly, the call to prayer that echoes across the muslim world, now thousands of miles away, or the distant notes of a piano fill us with a longing for our particular idea of home. The smells and sounds have become such a part of us that they cannot be separated from our life story.

At other times familiar actions transport us home. Whenever I walk into my parent's apartment I start shuffling through their mail, connecting with people and places that represent home. Mom and dad seem to understand. They never chide me for not respecting their privacy. In the absence of a physical childhood home that I can return to, this reconnecting through paper is important. Our conversation, as I rummage, is of family friends they have recently heard from, or recent events in Pakistan that have come to their attention.

"It is the sounds we hear as children that shape us" writes Saadia Shepard at the start of *The Girl From Foreign*. Shepard's book is a journey about finding home. Raised in Massachusetts, daughter of a Pakistani mother and an American father, Shepard heads to Bombay on a Fulbright Scholarship to research the childhood home of her beloved grandmother. Her story has gotten into my bones and resonated with my soul. Her journey, like mine, is a journey of living between worlds, searching for identity, discovering 'home.'

I read in Psalm 84: "Blessed are those whose strength is in you, who have set their hearts on pilgrimage… They go from strength to strength until each appears before God in Zion." In my journey, this Psalm makes *"Home is where your suitcase is"* a spiritual reality. The Psalmist says nothing about the concept, idea, or definition of home. But the Psalm speaks to the blessing of pilgrimage and the strength that comes with the journey.

Monsoon Rains

Each year by mid-July the monsoon rains would arrive in Murree. We would go from glorious sunshine and fields of daisies to soggy puddles, torrential rain and a fog that enveloped the mountainside and rushed into the house whenever you opened the door.

The monsoon rains were like nothing I've ever seen in the West. They would soak you through in minutes. Clothes and houses were perpetually damp and smelled of mildew. Shoes, if left in the closet for too long, would turn green with mold. The makings of penicillin were all around us.

When the monsoons came it was easy to believe that a flood could wipe out the whole earth.

My mom would try without success to dry our laundry by setting up makeshift clothes lines all over our small living quarters. Life was perpetually humid and moist.

The school we attended was an old church building with a tin roof. The rain would come without warning on school days, beginning with a pitter-patter and ending with a roar. Classes were known to stop because the teacher, even shouting, could not compete with the sound of the monsoon rain on the tin roof. Buckets placed throughout the classroom created an obstacle course, there to collect the rain that would sometimes drip and other times pour through cracks in the ceiling.

Despite these weeks of fog, the discomfort of sticky, damp clothing, and the ever-present scent of mildew competing with the strongest of perfumes, these monsoons were an expected part of life, understood and tolerated. Monsoon rains meant water for the rest of the country. Monsoon rains meant good harvests in places far away.

The rains also meant landslides and tragedies, occasional floods and internally displaced people. Rain was life – the good and the hard, the beautiful and the terrible.

The rain on the tin roofs would fall through July and August, but just as you could count on its coming, you could also count on the monsoon leaving, giving way to glorious sunshine and clear views of some of the highest mountains in the world.

Rain was the sound of home and belonging. As a small child I would wake to thunder and lightning, followed by torrential rainfall. I was rarely afraid – rather I would clutch my covers close to my chin, say a silent prayer and drift off to sleep to a land of sunshine and hope.

It's strange that after all these years I would think about rain on a tin roof. Some moments stay with you forever, not because they are particularly deep or noble but because they were such a constant in the life that shaped you. A continuous thread in the thick tapestry of events woven together to shape the life that is yours.

Hawke's Bay

Every winter for one week our family would take a vacation to the Indian Ocean on the Karachi coast. A small, two-room hut just steps from an open sandy beach was our haven for that week. Throughout the years, this beach hut saved many a missionary from lasting emotional damage.

With no running water or electricity and old furniture, refurbished just enough for comfort, the beach hut was nothing short of magical.

We would drive all day from upper Sindh to Karachi. Leaving before the sun came up, before the call to prayer. We were able to drive for miles before brightly painted trucks transporting goods across the country slowed us down.

The first stop would be Empress Market in Karachi. Coming from upper Sindh, this market was an amazing display of goods with fresh produce, meat, canned goods, and store bought butter. Buying both treats and staples, we would arrive at the beach hut with a week's worth of food.

Leaving the bustling city of Karachi behind we traveled down a long road lined with royal palm trees. Each kilometer brought us closer to the ocean. We could not wait to arrive.

It was usually late afternoon as we pulled up in our Landrover to unpack, wanting to finish quickly so we could claim our beds. Walking inside we could see the ocean and the salty air would waft through the open windows reviving us in an instant.

That first night we would eat a feast fit for a royal family and play games in the light of a pressure lantern.

Each day ended with my mother reading to us. Through the sound of her voice and the skill of the book's author we traveled to British Columbia, Canada with a small boy orphaned and living with his grandmother; to the busy streets of a Jewish community in Brooklyn, New York; to a farm in an English countryside and a little city girl who coped poorly with the changes that had come her way. We fell asleep to the sounds of the ocean and my mom's voice.

Each day we were up early. None of us could sleep for the excitement of the ocean and all it held. For six days we were held captive by sand, sun, sand castles, ocean water, games of fox and goose, and catching ocean crabs that scurried across the flat sand. The most magical activity of all – watching baby sea turtles hatch and dig their way out of the hole made so carefully by their mamas, making the long and potentially treacherous journey from nest to ocean. We would ward off predators that came from far and wide to try and catch their prey – a morsel of tiny turtle. The turtles had to work hard to get to the ocean. It was years after that we found out that this journey from nest to sea was pivotal in preparing and strengthening them for a life at sea in what would be a hostile environment for these beautiful and innocent sea creatures.

The spiritual lesson, even at an early age, was not lost on

me. The journeys that these turtles made, preparing them for their life ahead held parallels to my journey in boarding school and the safety of a small community before I was cast into the ocean of the world, where my environment sometimes turned hostile.

Each year, my father would pick one day during the week to go 'bunder boating' – deep sea fishing. We would head out to the ocean from a nearby fishing village. My mother never came on these trips. I realize as an adult that this was probably one of her favorite days of the year, a day when she was alone and at peace by the ocean. When she could think, write, and pray, preparing her for the year ahead that was certain to hold the unexpected and call on all of her God-given strength to cope.

All too soon our week would come to an end.

We cleaned the sand out of the hut, leaving it as clean as we could for the next family who would come. An old guest book chronicled the visits of others, each entry original but all attesting to the magic of Hawke's bay.

To this day many of us would say that Hawke's Bay, in all its rustic simplicity was the best vacation spot on God's earth.

Kebabs in Jalalabad

Mouth-watering chunks of lamb and fat on skewers cooked on live coals, served with hot Kabuli *naan* and strong sweet tea. It sounds like a menu item from an expensive ethnic restaurant in New York City or another world-class destination. Instead, it is straight out of a highway restaurant off the Khyber Pass, the pass linking Pakistan and Afghanistan that twists and winds its way through the Hindu Kush mountain range, banked by perilous cliffs.

I was last in Jalalabad before the Soviet invasion of Afghanistan, and just prior to the military takeover that set the stage for it. More than forty of us, high school students and accompanying staff members, stopped for a much-needed break from a long bumpy bus ride through the pass from Peshawar. We welcomed the food and talk around the table before a late night arrival in Kabul. Amidst all of the momentous events that have occurred since that time, in Pakistan, Afghanistan and my life, this memory has stayed with me.

It is fitting that this city, so strategic in trade and transportation between Pakistan and Afghanistan, should serve up one of the finest meals I have tasted in a setting void of crystal and candles. It is also interesting that memories of these times for a third culture kid are so intense and clear despite the time that has passed.

The losses felt by those of us raised in a country that was different from that indicated on our passports can be heavy. To be sure, the gains are also real: The way we look at the world, the wonder of travel, our love of passports and places, our wish to defend parts of the world that we feel are misunderstood by those around us.

But along with these come profound losses of people and place. For many of us, the only thing we feel we have left are our memories. We cannot go back to the place that was home. Either it does not exist, will not let us in, or danger and cost prohibit a casual trip to indulge the times of homesickness. In its place is memory. Our memories may be biased, or relayed in a way that our mothers would say, "That's not quite the way it happened," but it is inalienably ours.

The circumstances beyond our control that contribute to these losses may be easy to explain – graduation from high school or the need to take A-Level exams in the UK – or they could be more complicated and painful, a mother's diagnosis of breast cancer or a father's death or indiscretion. Through all the change that accompanies our moves, our memories console us as we struggle, just as immigrants do, to adapt to our new world and surroundings. And so, in the midst of all of transition and loss, I shut my eyes and remember the taste of kebabs in Jalalabad.

The Train Party

In 2011 *The International Business Times* published an article marking the 150th anniversary of the railway system in northwestern India, now Pakistan:

> *On May 13, 1861, the first engine left the station in Karachi to an astonished crowd. One of a kind in the region, locals were shocked as John Brunton, the Chief Engineer of the Karachi-Kotri Railway, drove the steam locomotive for its first trial. "The Karachi natives were astounded," Brunton recalled, "I drove the engine myself of course at slow speed - the natives thronging all around, I was fearful of some accident. At last, I thought I should frighten them away, so I blew the engine steam whistle loudly. Instantly, they all rushed back from the 'Demon' falling over one another.*

I smiled as I read. Train travel and my childhood go hand in hand. My earliest memories include the rhythmic sound of train engines chugging their way through the countryside of Pakistan. Even now when I close my eyes on the subway en route to an ugly, institutional grey building in the heart of Boston, the rhythm of the train transports me back to another time and place.

When my parents arrived in Pakistan in 1954 trains were the most common way to get from place to place in the country. Train travel was safe, cheap, and relatively comfortable.

Those of us who lived in the south of Pakistan traveled north by train to our boarding school. Families organized, banded together and sent chaperones on a train with their school-age children for the twenty-four hour journey to Rawalpindi. On arrival, the school sent their solid army-green school bus, bearing the name and emblem of Murree Christian School, to the station to take us the rest of the way to the school. The trip was affectionately called The Train Party.

I was seven when I first joined my older siblings for The Train Party. I had heard it mentioned so many times that the images in my mind had taken over. A Party! Games! Food! Friends! What could be better? I had dreamt of the day I would join the ranks of missionaries' children heading off to school. The Train Party was a rite of passage. We arrived at the station with trunks, small carry cases, and *bisters*, large green canvas carriers stuffed with bedding. Our moms had lovingly hand prepared food for us, hearts aching as they packed sandwiches, cookies, and carrot sticks.

I stood nervously with my older brothers, aware that this was a big moment. Already I felt a shyness come over me in relation to these brothers with whom I lived, played, ate and fought with. I somehow knew that The Train Party would usher us into a different world, a world where it was not easy to acknowledge siblings, where home and family connections grew more distant with each station and each rhythmic sound of the wheels on the track.

The Party began in Hyderabad. As the train made stops

along the way, snaking its way from the Sindh desert to the lush Punjab, children of various ages and sizes joined us. We were a motley assortment. Meg, Lizzie and David from the UK; Nancy, David, and Jonathan from Atlanta; Bill, Paul, Phil and Tim, four brothers from the Midwest, whose mother I loved; Alberteen Vanderveen from Holland.

Sometimes we had moments of extraordinary excitement. "Help, someone's lost a thumb!" The cry rang through the compartments during one train party. We all looked in horror at our own, now precious, thumbs. The Someone had been on the top bunk of the compartment, near the small fans that whirred dangerously close to heads to keep air circulating. She had accidentally reached up during a shaky point in the normally smooth ride, lopping the tip of a thumb off. Blood flowed freely, making the accident appear far worse than it was.

A thumb was not the only thing lost as the train sped its way north through brown desert and green fields. Hard-boiled eggs, carrot sticks that dried in the arid air, trash that we hadn't yet learned should be disposed of properly were lost intentionally, furtively thrown out the window. Other things, like sleeping bags and a favorite sweater, were lost unintentionally. Once we almost lost Lizzie Hover. She leaned out the window, so far that we had to pull her back to safety. In a rare moment of selflessness, my imagination went wild with the grief her mom would feel at the loss of Lizzie.

The long train ride provided time to reconnect with friends, who like us had spent their winters isolated from one another in towns throughout the country. At stations we bought hot tea, *pooris* and *halwa*. Shouts of *"Chai, chai, garam chai"*(Tea, tea, hot tea!) and *"Undae, undae, garam undae"*(Eggs, eggs, hot eggs!) were heard at every stop. Station food tasted to us like gourmet cuisine.

The trip ended just as it became unbearable for the adults. We were unloaded from the train, only to be packed into the school bus for the last two hours of the journey to Murree, where we would begin the spring term.

The first evening in Murree was full of chaos and excitement. Unpacking began. We were allowed to stay up later than our normal, strictly enforced bedtimes, and we began to claim drawers, dressers, and beds. I don't remember much fighting. This was a new beginning and we were excited to be together again. The night ended with a meeting in our houseparent's apartment. The meeting closed with prayer and we traipsed to our rooms, ready, finally, for a night's sleep in a real bed on solid ground.

I never failed to wake up early the next morning, disoriented as soon as I opened my eyes, not knowing where or who I was. As I slowly woke to my reality, tears would well. I was not unhappy to be there. But I had left the safety of the unconditional love of parents and home. I was in a place where my daily world was full of those as immature as I. As much as I loved her, my substitute mother for the next three months would be a houseparent, with many others to care for, all away from their moms, all needy of a mother's love, care, and patience.

As I wept silently an invisible strength seemed to enter me. God himself seemed to speak to me through my tears, "I am here, I am here for you." Those words, whispered in the early morning, were stronger than any sermon or theological discussion could be, taking root deep in my sub-conscious giving me strength to get up and begin the new semester.

Chai, Chai, Garam Chai!

I was raised on chai. Not the fake chai, branded by corporate money-makers and changed into an expensive, frothy *"I'll take a chai latte."* Instead it was real chai. Rich and creamy, made with strong Lipton Gold Label loose leaf tea, sugar, and rich water buffalo milk. I learned before I entered kindergarten that this drink could get me through many trials in life. It was not just the taste; it was the full experience of comfort that nourished body and soul.

My memories of chai span my developmental stages. They begin with childhood when chai was poured from a chipped teacup into the saucer to cool it down before drinking so it would not scald the throat. In boarding school chai was the comforting breakfast and teatime drink served immediately after school. No matter what the day held, whether a chiding from a teacher, or a bout of homesickness, the time set aside for a cup of chai would put life in perspective. There were times when many of us felt that the only nutritional value we were receiving was from our daily dose of chai. Who needed vitamins or other nutrients when you could satisfy yourself with steaming hot goodness in a cup?

I moved on to seeing chai as an essential ritual in the life of a teenage girl who liked a boy. Saturday and Sunday nights provided opportunities for eye-heart connections in the chai shops of the thriving non-metropolis of Jhika Gali. There our teenage angst found an outlet in drinking chai and talking for as many hours as we were allowed, sometimes outside overlooking the foothills of the Himalayan mountain range and other times with as many as would fit squished around a small table inside the shop. I would love to interview the teashop owners now and see what stories they could tell of this motley group of children from many different countries and language groups all gathered sharing a common bond of life in boarding school in Pakistan, with chai as a staple.

Just as the sound of the call to prayer lets me know that I am in a familiar place I can call home, so does the sound of *"Chai, chai garam chai"* (Tea, tea, hot tea!) belted out in melodious tones at a train station signify that I am in a comfort zone of sorts. A zone where memories abound and my adult life, sometimes just a bit too complicated for my liking, can take a back seat to the warm and delicious memories and taste of chai.

The Mango

The *New York Times* calls them the King of Fruits and declares they should command respect in the food world. The comments are effusive. *Mango my friend, nectar of Heaven. Divine Fruit. The fruit that inspired the Moghul poets! 450 varieties of mangoes in Pakistan.* All I can see in the pictures are yellow shapes, each one showing a different texture.

As I look, the memories and the emotions the pictures elicit are far more than mangoes. I hear the fan whirring above me from the twenty-five foot high ceiling of our home. I hear the muted voices outside the walls, Urdu, Punjabi, and Sindhi all blending into one sound just steps from my door. I smell the sawdust put down on the floor earlier in the morning to allow the dust that settles daily to be swept up from chipped marble or concrete floors. I see the buffalo milk, delivered earlier by the milkman, now boiling away in the kitchen, leaving a thick rich cream that will later be made into butter, and leftovers that will be whipped into a cream to put over stewed guavas. I smell *dahl* and rice or *keema* curry simmering on the stove, the spices wafting through the air. I see myself, curled up on a *charpai*, legs tucked under me, reading Chaim Potok's *The Chosen*.

Mangoes evoke the timelessness of my childhood, when I seldom felt rushed, when I could eat mangoes undisturbed, unembarrassed by the juice dribbling down my chin. But my mango days have passed. In their place are hurried times and harried thoughts. Instead of taking the time to peel a mango and sit eating it, marveling at its taste and smell, I buy the little frozen pieces of mango contained in a twenty four ounce package from Trader Joe's, often forgetting to defrost them ahead of time. Or I spend a day's food budget on a half-ripe mango purchased in a place where produce is put into little plastic packets and wrapped in cellophane, to keep me from touching, feeling or smelling.

Only occasionally am I fortunate enough to find that perfect mango and I let the taste and everything it evokes fill me once again.

The Chai Shop

As young women growing up in Pakistan our rite of passage at boarding school was getting into high school and being able to go to the 'Chai Shop.'

The Chai Shop stood across from the front gates of the school. It was small and dark inside with a couple of wooden tables, rickety chairs and an old stove.

What did this 'rite of passage' entail? It meant that at morning break and lunch time you had the freedom to go a few yards across the street and sit with friends, talking, laughing and drinking chai. There we would sit, sipping from cups, sometimes burning our tongues from the steaming hot drink. We were oblivious to anything outside of our sphere, content to just be. It was a delight.

The Chai Shop had rickety steps and blackened walls, old tables and wood smoke. It had chipped china cups and grungy floors. It had an old stove and an owner who welcomed us. The Chai Shop was full of the smell of frying *ghee* and boiled milk, spicy omelettes and sweet, semi-stale rolls. It was full of comfort and belonging all wrapped up in a package right outside our doors.

I've heard that our boarding school now has tall walls around it with armed men standing guard, security measures put in place after a terrorist attack that took the lives of a couple of staff members and caused trauma in many others. Times have changed and we all know that. Pakistan is no longer the country we grew up in.

We are not those teenagers anymore either. We are now adults with history behind us. Life is far more complicated and has held its share of joys and sorrows. Some of our relationships have remained strong, and when we see each other we pick up where we left off. Other relationships are gone forever, into the faded photographs in albums and year books, and the rare smiles that memories evoke.

I've written before that there can be strength in remembering. And the Chai Shop is a memory that gives strength. It leaves no bitter after taste, no sad longing. Instead the memory remains just as it should – a rite of passage for a group of third culture kids, who had not yet found their way in the wider world but were growing into adults that would soon face a new rite of passage. A rite of passage that would take all the strength and fortitude that a good cup of chai and a solid upbringing can give — that of entry into the countries identified on the covers of those legal documents that supposedly confirmed our identity, otherwise known as our passports.

Rumor has it that the building that housed the chai shop has been torn down – one more brick taken out of our wall of memories. Perhaps writing helps keep some of the bricks intact, because memories are precious and if used properly give strength for the present.

Burqas & Miniskirts

The setting: Murree. The scene: a boarding school dormitory. Lead character: Me. The conflict? The dress code.

For those who grow up "between worlds," tension is inevitable. The tension can vary year-to-year or day-to-day, depending on the context, the issue, and even their age. At any given time, my world was either at peace or in conflict.

In junior high, conflict came through that dog-eared vehicle of Western thought and fashion, the JC Penney catalogue. Each of us pored over the Penney's catalogue until it was time to pass the treasure on to the next person. And Penney's brought us into direct conflict with the Dress Code.

We lived in a conservative society. As young women, we knew that we could go nowhere alone, and we fully understood the rule. There were no compliance problems. Away from school, in our homes, we formed friendships with women already veiled and with girls approaching puberty who would soon be wearing their first *burqa*. Many of us comfortably wore the traditional *shalwar kameez*. We appreciated the flow and texture of beautiful fabric, the way fashions changed, the joy of shopping in the *zenana* (women's) sections of a *bazaar*.

But in Murree we were not home. We were in boarding school. We knew that in the West mini-skirts were fashionable. And that is what we wanted. The dress code specified that a dress had to reach the floor when we were kneeling. For teenage girls, uneasily poised between worlds, this was an open invitation to rebel. We wanted mini-skirts and we would fight, or scheme, to wear them. To outwit the ever-present, ever-vigilant-about-length-of-skirts staff members, we became adept at the "quick hem," taking needle and thread to dresses too long and raising the hemlines with large and messy stitches that were easily ripped out at a moment's notice. Some of us even resorted to wearing calf-length coats, our bare knees poised to peek out at an approaching boy.

Music was another area of conflict. At a time when Umm Kulthum's songs crooned with mournful hope on radios in Cairo, and *ghazals*, *Saraiki* music, and *Bhangra* were heard throughout the areas of Pakistan where we lived when we were home, our boarding school was alive with the Beatles, Fleetwood Mac, the Beach Boys, and Creedence Clearwater Revival. Disguising the covers of cassette tapes to make them seem benign to the observant boarding parents became an art form and allowed us freedom from censorship. We took advantage of the cultural illiteracy that inevitably develops in adults who are both away from their home countries and the latest trends and removed by age and generation from pop culture. "Oh Cecilia, you're breakin' my heart, you're shakin' my confidence daily" blared out at camping trips and in dorm rooms, the volume turned down as the song moved on to "Makin' love in the afternoon, with Cecilia," and raised again once a teacher or boarding parent had moved on to the next room, convinced of compliance and innocence, or maybe just unable to catch the more devious among us in the act.

Every good story has a conflict. Never being fully part of any world is ours. This is what makes our stories and memories rich and worth hearing. We live between worlds, sometimes comfortable in one, sometimes in the other, but only truly comfortable in the space between. This is our conflict and the heart of our story.

Baby Switching

In a world of movement, I am grateful to have some Forever Friends, friends who I am immediately comfortable with no matter how much time has passed. My childhood friend, Maylene, is one of them. We were raised in Pakistan, walked through life together until we turned eighteen, and graduated, leaving behind the 'known' and the comfortable.

Our history began with two confused fathers and two irate mothers. During the summer season in Pakistan, families would flock to places that offered cooler temperatures, an escape from the oppressive heat of southern areas in the country. Murree was one such escape. Situated at 7500 feet above sea level and about fifty kilometers from the capital, Islamabad, it was a popular hill station, and was filled with lively activity throughout the summer. Many missionary families would come to the area and set up temporary housing, the fathers staying in the southern region completing work, the mothers taking their children out of boarding school and living in small cottages dotting the hills surrounding the town.

The church nursery at Holy Trinity Church on Mall Road in Murree Hills, Pakistan was a bustling place as missionary families did not shirk the mandate in Genesis to "Be fruitful and multiply." Maylene and I were less than a month apart. I was born at the end of January and she came in mid-February. Both of us had baby-soft dark hair and dark eyes. We could have been no more than a few months old when our distracted fathers, Bill and Ralph, sent to pick up their babies from the nursery, walked in and each picked up a baby they supposed was theirs.

Only when they were halfway to their respective summer homes on the hillside, probably through a telltale cry, did our mothers realize there had been a terrible mistake. I can only imagine what they felt as they looked, horrified, at the babies in the arms of their husbands, realizing at once that it was the wrong child. How could we not be friends after such a beginning?

Our friendship stayed strong through babyhood, toddlerhood, and kindergarten. Maylene was the athlete and artist; I had the voice. We both had dark hair that was short or long in accordance with style or our moms' preferences. We went on through elementary school, playing steal the bacon; middle school, playing steal the boy; and high school, playing steal the show. Every year we were roommates at boarding school and weathered the storms, sometimes hurricanes, of childhood.

When middle-school angst came, we bonded together despite boys and houseparents who threatened to break us apart. Senior year we were the only girls in the class and went through the year elated at our 'senior' status, all the while knowing that our world was soon to end. And it did end in July of 1978, when, through tears and promises, we parted, Maylene to California, me to Chicago. I sang at her wedding in Abbotabad in 1980; In July of 1984 she flew in to Chicago with her two toddlers to attend mine. We have never again been mistaken for each other. We haven't even lived in the same city. But we both have five kids, pierced noses, strong memories of a shared history, a creative bent, and a great many opinions. And when we happen to be in the same city or country we get together and share life just as we did so many years ago in a church nursery.

Thirty-Six Years

It has been thirty-six years. Thirty-six years since we shared the same bedroom, listened through louvered windows to the sounds of mountain breezes and birds, slept on gray, drab, metal beds lent personality only by the bedclothes, shared crowded dressers, six drawers each, reserving precious space for those special knickknacks that defined us.

Thirty-six years since we dated Tim and Skip, walked to and from the small village chai shop full of hope and longing, holding hands until the lights from an oncoming car would sever the chemistry that raced through our bodies. Thirty-six years since Friday morning chapel and afternoon tea, trips to the town of Murree for shopping and late night conversations. Thirty-six years since we were young and life seemed simpler, wrapped up in our third culture belonging that held us tight.

Junior year she left while I stayed. She went back to Small Town, USA. I remained in Pakistan, experiencing all the things that senior year brought: Senior Skip Day (weekend really), Banquet, being the oldest in the small school that we called home, and finally the pinnacle of our time at Murree, Graduation, with all its pomp and circumstance, speeches, musical numbers, and tears.

A lot of life has happened. A lot of good and a lot of hard. Meeting my beautiful friend outside a restaurant in the middle of Central Massachusetts was a whole lot of good.

The bonds forged during those early years in Pakistan are strong like steel, hard to bend, impossible to break. Politics, religious beliefs, lifestyles - none of that matters as I hug my friend. Right there I'm back in Murree, laughing over monkey turds and gross milk, crying over stupid boys and the mandatory "greenie" gym uniforms, designed to be ugly enough to repel any potential admirer.

We hug tightly. The picture we take is terrible, but she assures me her husband will take more later. It is all so natural. It is all so easy. We don't have to explain stuff. We go straight to the 'hard,' the easy small talk does not work.

We don't have to explain boarding school or Pakistan; plane rides or missionary parents; bazaar bargaining or why we love a part of the world that is only bad news in the media. We don't have to search for words to describe 're-entry'and 'adjustment,' the pain of the search to belong or being 'other.' It is all a part of our 'tribal' language, our shared experience.

Too soon, it is time to leave. But I am lucky. She will be in my area for a couple more years. There will be more time. More stories. More life.

Third culture kid reunions are like no other. I leave full, the ride home is a ride of hope and nostalgia. And I reenter my world utterly thankful for my past and rejoicing in my present. I cling to the heritage I have, the people who have loved and walked beside me and the recognition that memorials are made of stone or steel or granite and real life is made of flesh and blood, tears and smiles, sorrow and joy.

34

Klondike Avenue

In 1969 our family left Pakistan for a year in the United States. We rented a home on Klondike Avenue in Fitchburg, Massachusetts. It couldn't have been a better place for our family of seven. We had space and safety in a medium-sized industrial city in New England. We were minutes from my parents' home church and the neighborhood epitomized the words 'family friendly.'

Klondike Avenue was thousands of miles away from our world in Pakistan. We traded boarding school for day school, a diesel Land Rover for a Ford station wagon, Sunday night singspirations for Sunday night cereal. We were the missionary family with all the kids, and everyone in the neighborhood seemed to know we were coming.

The day we arrived, Carin Waaramaa came to the door of our house. She had come to invite me, a stranger, into her world. Even at age nine Carin was a beauty. She had her mom's curly hair and her eyes sparkled under eyelashes a mile long. She was taller than me and slender. Carin and I could talk for hours, and during that year on Klondike Avenue we were inseparable. We walked to school every morning, talked about our mutual crush on Daryl Freeburg, timidly entered into cheerleading for the church basketball team, and watched the end of *Dark Shadows* on a small television high on the wall of a dingy lobby at the YMCA after weekly swimming lessons.

Neither Carin nor I had ever heard the term third culture kid. I had no label, came with no warning sign and certainly no instruction manual.

To Carin I was just Marilyn. And when the year ended our goodbye was one of the hardest I would say. We never lived in the same place again, and time and life moved us far away from that year on Klondike Avenue. Carin was my first childhood friend to die. She died too young, leaving two young children, her extended family, and a mom who exemplifies grace and compassion.

Klondike Avenue was Carin Waaramaa, East Street School, swimming in the Pierce's pool and playing softball on late spring evenings on the field above Rodney Pierce's house. It was riding bikes to the book mobile that came every Thursday and Vacation Bible School at Highland Baptist Church. Klondike Avenue was a four bedroom house and dandelions on a long, sloping front lawn; it was instant friendships and a gaggle of kids. Most of all it was the Waaramaa and Schotanus families, the Pierce families times three, and us, the Brown family. For a kid coming from Pakistan, Klondike Avenue was near perfect.

A year ago I returned to Fitchburg for a meeting. As I followed my carefully printed directions, heading up the steep hill to the old Burbank Hospital, now a community health center, I suddenly felt a familiar tug on my brain and heart. I couldn't place it. Then there it was, Klondike Avenue, right in front of me.

36

When I want to be critical of the United States, when my heart goes to a place of alienation and feelings of misunderstanding, I sometimes close my eyes and think of Klondike Avenue. For Klondike Avenue gave us, a missionary family that needed rest, friendship, and belonging the best of the best, never asking for anything in return. Klondike Avenue was pure grace.

Rooted

For those who wear the third culture kid label and the Global Nomad tag proudly, the word 'rooted' is scary. For all we speak, ponder, and write of identity and crisis, for all we wistfully try to articulate what it means to belong, being 'rooted' can be terrifying.

Here are some myths that I have believed about being rooted: Being rooted means I'm from here. Being rooted means I can't leave. Being rooted means I'm stuck.

But perhaps being rooted gives strength. Perhaps being rooted doesn't mean I give up who I am; perhaps it means that I securely use my past as a bridge to my present. Rooted means I grow strong, like the sunflowers that are growing high in our garden, faces raised to the sun.

We often spend summer weekends in Rockport, Massachusetts — Rockport of the Motif #1, the most frequently painted structure in the United States, Rockport of the rocky coast and stunning gardens, Rockport of the artists and the creators, old inns by the sea, and marvelous sunsets.

Rockport is one of my favorite places on earth, ever.

For a woman who feels at home in the Middle East and Southeast Asia, who grew up fully comfortable with the call to prayer, who wears travel like she wears her favorite shoes and excitedly looks forward to trips to the airport taking her to far away places, this is a big deal.

The truth is that just as places in Pakistan have been a part of my life since I was a baby; there are places in New England that have also been a part of my life. That's the mystery of living in two worlds.

And Rockport is one of those places. I can't remember when I first visited; all I know is that it has long been a place of peace, rest, and beauty, a place where time stops and all life feels rooted.

My love of Rockport reached a new level a few years ago when we took a risk and bought a condominium a block from the rocky seacoast. We convinced ourselves that we could rent it out during the school year and use it during the summer months. This way it would not be a financial burden during a time when we needed to focus on other priorities. Every year at least once, I think to myself, "Perhaps we need to sell our condo in Rockport." But the thought is quickly swatted out of my head like an annoying mosquito.

Sell Rockport? No! For in our life of many moves this feels steady and solid. After twenty-nine years of marriage and seventeen houses, the entire family desperately needs a Rockport. We need to know there is a place that isn't going away soon.

We know that nothing is permanent, what we need to be able to say is that some things are steady, some things can be solid. Our memories are precious reminders that we have developed roots. They may not go very deep, but they are still firm. They may be pulled up rudely, but not without a fight.

Identity

Turns out identity isn't about a place you live at, but a Person you live in.

Chameleon

"You're like a chameleon," said my friend. "You change according to the situation; according to whom you are around!" And, finally, six horrible, crushing words: "You don't know who you are!" I was dumbfounded and tearful.

I imagined myself to be easy-going and compatible, but I had just been likened to a chameleon, changing in seconds depending on who was in my immediate vicinity overshadowing my real colors. The flexibility that I had learned at a young age, and that I thought I wore so well, was now marking me as a cold-blooded reptile that changed according to the world around it, but was never fully a part of that world. The same ability to change and adapt to my circumstances that seemed to serve me so well in my growing up years in Pakistan, and then again as an adult in Egypt, put me in the family of a six-inch long chameleon, someone who changes behavior and identity in response to environment. My friend had accused me of being an impostor, fabricating who I was to become what others wanted, taking on a false personality in order to deceive.

There was truth in what my friend was saying. I honestly didn't know who I was. How could I? I didn't have the capacity to live effectively and honestly in my present world while continuing to care for and be true to the world I had left, and loved, so well and so long. The self-reflection was good. There had to be a way to make this work. Others had gone before me. How had they negotiated this "between worlds" dilemma?

How could I move beyond myself to use those "best of skills" that are present in third culture kids? The adaptability, the interest in the world at large, the telling of stories, the tolerance of ambiguity, the knowledge of pain and what it feels like to be "other"?

Any third culture kid who is living effectively in her passport country has a moment of truth when she realizes it's okay to live here; it's okay to adjust; it's okay, even if she never feels fully at home, to feel a level of comfort in who she is in her passport country. To adapt doesn't mean settling for second best. To adapt is to use the gifts she developed through her childhood in order to transcend cultures and to find her niche in both worlds.

A sentence in *Unrooted Childhoods* by Faith Eidse and Nina Sichel articulates those things that can come to signify home and roots for children torn from their geographical roots: "Family, religion, language, memories carried within, become the home these children are unable to return to, a home not defined by geography."

As for my identity and roots journey? As I was writing this, I read these words: "Turns out 'safe' isn't a place you live at — but a Person you live in." Altering two words captures my experience: Turns out *identity* isn't about a place you live at — but a Person you live in.

Impostor

There was a time when we didn't have a name. When we were forever told to pull up our bootstraps and get on with life.

There was a time when we thought we were the only ones, traveling solo in our passport countries, not knowing how to put words to our longings, how to verbalize our pain.

There was a time when reentry seminars were non-existent and it was assumed that we would arrive in our passport countries without incident, when folks said to us "Aren't you glad to be back home" and we nodded assent, while a part of us shriveled inside. We would assimilate, and no one would ever know that part of us that shaped and molded us from birth.

There was a time when we over spiritualized and downplayed 'place' and 'home,' convincing ourselves that since our real home was in Heaven, earth really didn't matter too much. But ah, when we got to Heaven that would all change. Except that we were young and Heaven seemed oh so far away.

There was a time when we failed to understand that throughout history, God has used place. There was a time when we laughed at the thought that we had losses, we brushed away any grief. "That's ridiculous," we sniffed! Other's have far more losses. Others are far worse off. But then we faced one too many moves and in the back of our minds, the whisper of losses began to shout.

And then someone invented a name, a name with a thousand meanings and memories. We became third culture kids. And we learned that we were not alone, that there were so many like us. We learned it was okay to have a name. It did not label us as an infection; it gave credibility to who we were and how we had lived. We were real. We could relax and begin to thrive. We had a place and we had a name — those Edenic characteristics applauded by God in the Garden so long ago. With a name we could grow into the people God intended us to be. And so we did.

Branded

I went to boarding school at age six. When I was in third grade a teacher asked me to stay after school. Being asked to stay after school rarely meant something good, usually it meant you were in some sort of trouble.

She waited until all the other children had left and then asked me to come to her desk. "You've been sick a lot" she said. Then she paused. "We all know you're faking so you need to stop being sick." My little 8-year-old heart stopped for a minute. Confusion and embarrassment flooded over my heart and face. Wait. What?

There was no "Can you tell me about how you feel? What you feel like when you're sick? Are you homesick? Do you miss your mom and dad? Do you miss your cat and rabbits?" No – none of that basic 'work with a child and figure out what's really going on' stuff. She was blunt and to the point and it worked. "You're sick, you're faking, you need to stop." That's it. Case closed.

When you're 8 years old and you're in boarding school there aren't many places to be alone. You room with six other little girls who are also far away from homes and mamas. You share meals with 60 to 100 other people in a large dining hall where bells signal the start and end to meals. You have devotions nightly with 20 pajama-clad girls, faces more or less washed and teeth sort of brushed. It is community living at its deepest, sometimes finest and sometimes worst, and most don't experience community living that early in life.

At age 8 you don't talk about coping or coping skills. You just go along with what happens. You're not unhappy, in fact often you're very happy. But after a couple of months it all gets to be a bit much. In my case I started out sick. I was truly sick with a fever and more. But yes, after realizing that being sick meant getting individual attention, getting sick meant being alone, getting sick meant special meals brought to you from the nurses infirmary — well then I thought it was something I wanted a bit more of.

As is wont to happen, some things make their way into the psyche and they stay there and rot. They become damaging. That is what happened with this interaction.

I was dismissed soon after and went up to the hostel, a short walk up stairs and across walkways on a slight incline. My loyal friends were waiting for me.

"What happened?"

"Why did you have to stay?"

"Are you in trouble?"

These were familiar words with boarding school kids. We functioned as a large, extended family and breaking rules or pushing margins was part of that. This time the words caught in my throat:

"She thinks I'm faking."

As I said it, the scarlet letter 'I' for impostor was branded hot on my soul.

48

I was an Impostor. I was a Fake. The damage went deep.

It wasn't helped by my natural chameliocity as a child raised between worlds. I was neither of one world, nor the other; I occupied a culture between. While in Pakistan I learned some Urdu, I embraced many things, I loved so much of the culture. But I stood out. I was not Pakistani.

In this other world called the United States, the blue passport bearing my picture and various stamps told me, told the world, that I belonged. I was a citizen. But I never felt like I belonged in this other world. At any given time I was less or more comfortable, but I always felt like a bit of a fake. I didn't know how to buy clothes. I didn't know how to dress for winter. I didn't know the idioms, the slang that was so important at that age. I had no clue about pop culture. I was trying to fake it, trying to fit, but at heart an impostor.

The scarlet letter continued to haunt me. When I experienced success or received an award, I felt, deep down, a sense that I did not deserve it, that someone would find out who I really was and the award, the success would be taken from me.

And then there was faith. In my Christian boarding school faith was applauded, but it was a non-denominational faith. We observed our parents and house parents working hard, transcending barriers of theological difference, emphasizing the Gospel essentials. I learned early in life that there were times when you had to 'agree to disagree' but that it didn't have to ruin friendships. Translating that experience to the Western church felt difficult. I felt that taking 'sides' was encouraged. If I didn't have a 'side,' I was a chameleon, wishy-washy.

"We know you're faking." I had internalized the words. No matter how successful I was, it would always come back to this. I was a fake. I was an Impostor. And someone would find out.

How are childhood word wounds removed? How is the tape rewound, erased, new words spoken that will move a third culture kid, or any child, forward into a new understanding of identity? How do you re-write the script to erase the scarlet letter from your heart and soul, replacing it with the seal of belonging?

Erasing the Scarlet Letter

I touched the top button on my grey sweater self-consciously. It was just about time for me to get up and address a group of women at a church retreat. It was Autumn and we were at a lovely camp on the shores of a lake in New England. The crisp air and brilliant red, orange, and gold of the leaves were reminders of why the season was so popular with tourists.

I was speaking about three women – a prostitute with a past, a queen with a purpose, and a teen with a pregnancy, Rahab, Esther, and Mary. And yes – I wanted to alliterate. I had prepared long and hard but still felt the butterflies of adrenaline and angst in my stomach.

I was introduced. I took a deep breath, mouthed a silent prayer and stepped forward. The talk went without a bump. I was clear, I connected, and I got good feedback. It was later during another talk that I suddenly realized I was still clasping my hands together tight, still had the butterflies, the angst. But it was no longer from adrenaline. What was it? As another woman began to speak on authenticity I suddenly realized why I was not at rest. I was terrified I would be thought a fake. I wasn't a Bible scholar. I had done little public speaking.

This was the first time I'd ever done something like this with a large group of women. In an instant I was eight years old and back in boarding school. I was looking up at a teacher and trying to absorb what she was saying.

I was back being branded with that indelible, scarlet 'I.' Impostor. Fake.

My tears burned inside my eyes and heart. I willed myself to stop them from spilling over onto my cheeks. "Erase the scarlet letter, take it away." The prayer was so deep I couldn't voice it. But suddenly I knew I had to. I had to speak out my pain, acknowledge the tape that had replayed over and over in my head since I was 8 years old. The tape screamed "You're an impostor, you're a fake." like a screeching song at high volume.

Soon after the woman invited us into an open space of vulnerability and I responded. As I began to speak the angst faded, in its place honesty and clarity. I told the boarding school story, spoke about the branding and how I hadn't realized how much it had influenced who I was, who I had become. I told of being called a chameleon, an impostor, wishy-washy when I thought I was just seeing and voicing different viewpoints. Acknowledged my fear as I prepared for the talk I had given earlier, fear that I would be discovered as a fraud. And I confessed, confessed to believing the lie instead of claiming truth.

And as I was speaking something remarkable happened. I realized that there was a far deeper brand on my heart, soul, and psyche than any childhood wound. It was the brand of belonging, the stamp of a King on his daughter.

I was God's. I was not fake to my Creator. I was real, flesh and blood with wounds that needed healing. I was His. No words could or would ever take that away. The scarlet 'I' was erased. In its place the glorious 'B' of belonging, a brand on my heart, a seal on my soul. The words of Psalm 139, always sweet to my soul, became sweeter.

> *My frame was not hidden from him, even when I was made in the secret place; when I was woven together in the depths of the earth. His eyes saw my unformed body and all the days ordained for me were written in his book before one of them came to be.*

Not only was the brand of belonging on my soul, my name was engraved on the palm of his hand, a sure symbol of God's love and mercy.

With that one act of honest obedience came healing. And what now? I still have residual effects of living so long with a lie. Those effects are not easy to erase. But a new script has been written, and I walk and live in that new script.

Rebranded in the Image of God

Some years ago an article in *Business Insider* looked at ten companies that successfully rebranded. They included Burberry, J.Crew, Old Spice, even McDonalds:

> The company that gave us transfat and that in abundance, now gives us little bags of sliced granny smith apples and salads. Old Spice cologne, previously for Old Men, gives us a handsome man on a black stallion. And Burberry, created for the man who goes fishing, has made plaid chic.

Why did they rebrand? A company rebrands in order to become more effective, to develop a new identity in the minds of consumers, to communicate a new message. It is hard work to rebrand a company and often takes a radical change in thinking, and in the way they do business. Its remarkable what successful rebranding can do.

And so it is with me. To rebrand takes a radical change in thinking: in the way I live, in the message I believe, in the message I communicate.

If mere humans can rebrand, how much more so can God who delights in restoring and rebranding? God who can work a radical change in his people, restoring his image for his glory.

Those childhood wounds that brand us, that tell us lies about who we are and what we'll become, are not strong when they come up against the Image of the God who made us. The impostor, the fake I believed myself to be was not a true brand, it told only a tiny part of the story. The real story came from before I was born, when I was knit in the womb. The real story came when on the day I was born, God saw what he had made and he called it 'Good.' The real story is not written in the things people say to us, the names we are called, or the hurts we've sustained; the real story is written in the work of God and his story of redemption and restoration, his story in our lives, and our story as it fits in with the Great Story.

So this impostor stuff? It may emerge now and then, filled with ugly and insecure, but it need never again define me, never again hold me hostage to memories. It will never make me believe that is who I am, that is what I am. I've been rebranded and I know I bear the stamp of the image of God, as powerful and secure an image as has ever been made.

Identity Theft

The day my passport expired and I realized there was no upcoming reason to renew it, I felt as if I had been robbed of my identity. Even Sandra Bullock in *While You Were Sleeping* had a passport, and she had not set foot outside the United States. At the time, I was in a Victorian house on the North shore of Boston living someone else's dream and someone else's life. I had known what a passport was since I was a tiny person. "Don't forget your passport" in our house was like "Don't forget to wash your hands" in other homes. But now I had no apparent need for what had always before been an essential.

My identity had already taken a beating. On moving back to the United States after a childhood and many years of adult life overseas, I quickly learned there were times where I needed to bite my tongue. Stories of dinner with Yasser Arafat's brother, or meeting with the Arab League proved to be conversation stoppers. When asked about my favorite restaurant I learned to pick a local establishment instead of saying, honestly, with eyes sparkling "The Menage. It's in Lahore." Or when playing two truths and a lie that I learned not to fall back on "I tasted my first strawberry in Afghanistan" or "I was conceived on the Queen Mary," instead settling for the more reasonable "I've been to Connecticut," or "I like to garden" (a lie). What to me was normal life experience, seemed alien and arrogant to others. I learned the hard way.

But by far the greatest difficulty with the biggest potential to rob me of my identity was the dreaded question "Where are you from?" I wanted to say "Pakistan" or "Egypt." But I knew I was not from Pakistan or Egypt. Sometimes the explanation would be too exhausting. As a child when I had voiced that response I was given blank looks or remarks like "Oh, do they wear clothes there?" True, the world has become more global since that time, but I still bear the memories of discomfort as I tried to think of a quick, snappy answer.

To the third culture kid, nothing immobilizes and challenges our identity like that question. What do you say? Do you claim your place of birth? The country where you spent the most time during your developmental years? The place where your parents grew up? During the time that you are internally asking yourself how to answer, your heart begins to beat faster and you feel your face growing hot. It makes no sense to the person asking the question. They cannot understand how this innocent question could produce these symptoms of discomfort.

Culturally "Where are you from" frames a large part of one's identity in the United States, so when we cannot answer the question, we are left with feelings of rootlessness and loneliness. We are unable to give the questioner a framework with which they are comfortable, instead forcing them to confront places that they don't know and where the media has had the upper hand in giving out misinformation.

My passport served as a comfort against those feelings, a reminder that the world was mine and my identity was solid. All I had to do was find my way to terminal E at Boston's Logan Airport with a credit card and my passport and I was ready to go. My passport was a validation, not of nationality, but of the bigger world that had shaped my life and cultural values. The stamped pages, indicating date and time of arrival and departure in countries worldwide, served as a legal document validating experiences that went beyond my appearance. The physical token of a current passport held so much meaning: identity, comfort, and anticipation.

My passport was my grown-up teddy bear. Its expiration was an identity theft of sorts, arousing a host of feelings for which I was unprepared. I was swept away in a tsunami of soul tears, tears that come from such a deep place that you do not think you can survive them. And in those soul tears, I made up my mind that no matter what, I would not let my passport expire again. While I knew that my identity was far more than a document that had expired, the symbol represented too much of my life – people I loved, places I had been and pivotal events that shaped who I had become – to let go. It was a crucial part of the complexity of my journey of identity.

No matter how old I get, no matter how little I will be traveling, no matter how expensive it is to renew, my passport will continue to be current and ready, a symbol of identity lost, but in time retrieved.

Belonging

When I finally stopped grasping at success, at confidence, at belonging, I inexplicably found it.....somehow that quest that felt like a burden on my back since boarding school days of popular groups and cliques, has slowly but steadily been broken. In some mysterious way, I belong.

Cairo Coffee Houses

Sitting in crowded outdoor coffee houses, drinking mint tea and partaking of the occasional *shisha*, talking for hours while time stands still – this is the Cairo coffee house. People watching, talking politics, reminiscing and bonding, the evenings during our recent trip stretched long into the night. Occasionally Backgammon emerged and two of the family played while the rest of us looked on.

It was as though time was nonexistent. We left when our eyes began to get heavy with happy exhaustion. The camaraderie and sense of belonging gave us a comfort that many never get to experience and we didn't want it to end.

These coffee houses in the East could teach the West much about community. In the West coffee shops are often about providing tables and computer space to individuals rather than catering to groups of people. In the West there is a hurried atmosphere – you need to order quickly, your debit card at the ready so that in a flash you can pay and get out of line, scrambling to find a seat in the process. You have dozens of choices – triple shot, double shot; latte, espresso; hazelnut, vanilla; large, venti; medium, grande; small, tall – it can be physically exhausting if you don't know how to speak coffee. Although I love coffee in the United States, I do not have endless time and I do not feel community.

A few years ago I read a study showing that three quarters of the world operates on a family and friend system of support; the remaining quarter operates on an institutional system of support. It is not surprising that the United States falls into the latter category. There are many things that institutions can do for us, but they can't provide the human connection for which we are hardwired. Family and friends give us this human connection and there is no place better to develop this connection than the Cairo Coffee House.

Cairo coffee houses with their steaming hot tea, the bright green leaves of fresh mint peeking out of the cup, or *ahwa masbut*, heaps of coarse white sugar on the side so you can sweeten to your liking are poured into glass cups that show the beautiful colors of the beverage choices. There are plenty of refills and the warmth goes through body straight to soul.

It's a false illusion to be sure, but when one relaxes in the wonder of Cairo coffee houses it's easy to feel that the Middle East is at peace.

Invisible Skills

As I reflect on my experience as a third culture kid and hear from others with similar backgrounds, it is clear that many of us face a common internal conflict between visible deficits and invisible skills. So glaringly visible are the deficits that casual passers-by will notice. But my appearance doesn't differ from many around me. I'm an invisible immigrant. My significant knowledge deficit is not accounted for. "You look the same. Therefore you should know. You should understand. You should respond the same."

No one looking at me guesses the turmoil and the cross-cultural "code-switching" going on in my brain and heart.

At one time or another I have been baffled by an ATM machine, paralyzed at the drive-through, and in the cereal aisle, confused by idioms, incapable of ordering at a restaurant, overwhelmed by the simple task of pumping gas, struggled to keep up with pop culture, ignorant of the answers to most of the categories in Trivial Pursuit, and confused at the "15 items and under" line in a store. What makes this more difficult is that all the skills that I used daily in the countries I call home (and others call foreign) are no longer useful. Instead, they have become invisible parts of me, parts that may never need to be used again. No one bargains for Granny Smith apples at the local grocery store. I've tried! The memories of the skill with which I navigated life overseas are juxtaposed against these feelings of inadequacy, and it is difficult to reconcile the two or to believe that I will ever become secure and confident in my new world.

I know how to find where Lego can be purchased in a country that has none. I can adapt a chocolate chip cookie recipe to taste good without brown sugar or chocolate chips. I can decode idioms in Arabic or Urdu. I am completely comfortable in crowded bazaars or navigating any major airport in the world. I can make an orange-cranberry salad without the cranberries. I have navigated labyrinths of government bureaucracy while still loving my adopted homeland. I have survived military take-overs, regional wars, and riots in the neighborhood. And I understand the importance of identifying friends with commissary privileges and making sure they are invited to dinner so that that next time I see them there will be cranberries for my orange-cranberry salad.

Sometimes I long to take those around me to my country and my place of comfort. I long to have our roles reversed so that I am the one helping them with sidelong glances of pity, giving them grace. At this point, I console myself with stories and memories, understanding that invisible doesn't mean absent.

Designed for Travel

Imagine if babies were born with the label 'Designed for Travel.' They would come equipped with strong bladders and stronger taste buds. They would have the ability to withstand high and low altitudes, hot and cold temperatures, and all in a twenty-four hour period. They would come with tiny baby suitcases that grew as they grew and contained all those things that go with the traveler's identity. Designed for Travel babies would be completely adaptable. They would have the ability to sleep in suitcases or on floors; in mom or dad's lap, or airport waiting areas, on airplanes or inland rovers. Neither hovercraft nor ferry would interrupt their rhythm, and moving trains would lull them to sleep. "Stranger Danger" warnings would be lost on them as they learned early on that the man in the turban was totally safe and would hold them and rock them when they cry. Or the strange woman being introduced as "Auntie" would soon be their favorite person.

Such babies would also come with the warning that once they become adults, the identity and label will not be removed. If they go for several months with no travel, they will surely rearrange furniture and spend hours on the internet searching for a job in some far off land, dreaming of airports and new destinations as their heads hit the pillow. They will write blogs entitled "Have Kids will Travel," and itch to get across international borders.

There is no doubt in my mind that some people are designed for travel. It is in their DNA. Even if they wanted to, they would be unable to change their cell structure or nucleus. It starts in the womb but there is no warning. This is the identity of the global nomad. We are "Designed for Travel" and through nature and nurture, it is a fact of our lives. While many find excitement in their first nine-to-five job with a good paycheck and benefits, those of us "Designed for Travel" wilt in what we perceive as the confines of a small grey cubicle. It is in those settings that they feel the life drain from them and struggle to articulate this to colleagues. When it comes to purchasing a home, the global nomad is initially terrified. "How on earth will this work with my global world?" they muse. "Can I really pin myself to a mortgage of thirty years?" Activities that bring security to others can make those designed for travel wary and insecure.

But those designed for travel also learn that despite location, their world can continue to thrive through books and friendships across the globe. They learn that no matter where they end up, no one can take away the designer label, it is written in indelible ink across their lives.

Pieces of Childhood

We recently cleaned our basement. Armed with energy and a dose of ruthlessness we tackled boxes and trunks, suitcases and containers. Woven through the piles was our life as a couple, then a family on three continents and in five states. Memories surfaced from as long ago as our newlywed days in Chicago and as recent as our most recent family home in Phoenix. As we worked through the piles, at every turn we found pieces of childhood, not ours but those of our adult children.

The stuffed dinosaur from *Land Before Time* benign and cuddly, a mockery of the extinct T. rex; a "Gotta get a Gund" teddy bear frayed around the ears; an Anne of Green Gables china doll purchased in Quebec City during a family vacation; American Girl dolls and hundreds of Lego bricks. There were drums and trophies, giant stop signs from the rooms of teenage boys, an old Snow White Halloween costume. Each piece of childhood evoked memories, told a narrative of toddlers and bedtime stories, reminded us of past events: An eleven year old, struggling to make sense of the foreign world of her passport country who burst into tears as she opened her birthday present and saw Samantha, an American Girl doll purchased in love despite no jobs and a lot of chaos; a toddler tucked into his bed with the teddy bear by his side, a clown in his hand and a thumb in his mouth; a teenager coming home at midnight with a speech trophy in his hands and a gleam in his eye.

These pieces are more precious because we moved far more than the average family. By the time my oldest was five she had lived in three countries and six houses. And while we made a home and hung our hearts wherever we found our suitcases, we lost some pieces along the way. We lost some ability to trust. We lost some security. We didn't know the meaning of roots.

We struggled silently even as outwardly we embraced change. We were the gregarious family with five kids who could seemingly handle everything. But some pieces were lost and there was an unspoken longing to try to get them back.

When pieces are lost, we struggle to find them again. When you move a lot it is easy to place your security in things, to begin to idolize place.

Where was God in all this? We had to learn that God was permanent despite our impermanence. We had to find God in the pieces, stepping out in faith that there would be a new community that could come along side us, that could help us put together the pieces. As a mom I had to learn that even all the king's horses and all the king's men couldn't put the pieces together. It had to be God. It has to be God.

All of this I thought of as I went through the containers and smiled at the tangled hair of dolls, no longer a part of the everyday world of their owner.

Pieces of childhood are important foundations to building adults. Whether it be the doll, the bear, or the book, its part of the story of our lives. The pieces of childhood bear witness to times and places that helped shape us into who we are today.

The basement is now clean and organized, sorted by kid and item. We've shut the door on those pieces until we can go through them again with our kids beside us.

And I walk away knowing that in the pieces of childhood there is grace and a Father God who delights in putting together the pieces.

Third Culture Kid Envy

An often-repeated quote among those who have lived overseas for extended periods goes like this: Spend a day in a country and you can write a book. Spend a week, you can write an article. Spend a lifetime, you can hardly write a sentence.

I recently picked up a book, full of seemingly intimate knowledge and details of a place, written by someone who has spent a bare fraction of a lifetime living overseas. Immediately I went to a dark place. What gives him the right to do this? What makes him think he has knowledge of the area? What makes him an expert? The questions running through my mind are judgmental, ugly, and colored with the horrible green of envy. I have succumbed once again to Third Culture Kid Envy Syndrome. Yes, this is a real thing, a real diagnosis made up by me. It is a diagnosis formulated through a lifetime of watching myself and others fall victim. It is a diagnosis that manifests in a tight chest, a seething rage that settles for just long enough to do damage, a hurt that cannot be described but can come across as a self-righteous know-it-all attitude. It is agonizing. And it is as real as any diagnosis in the Diagnostic and Statistical Manual of Mental Disorders (DSM).

Third culture kid envy is one of the consequences of being designed for travel. It is what I feel when my feet are trapped on the ground for too long while I watch others travel. It is what I feel when I hear others, sometimes worthy and sometimes not, talk about Pakistan or Egypt, my beloved places. It is what I taste when I hear that someone is going on a long trip, leaving from the international terminal just minutes from my house. It reaches crisis stage when I find out someone is moving overseas. And I so long and need to overcome this syndrome, but there are times when I think that is impossible.

I wish I could find the remedy in a little purple, blue, or white pill but I cannot. Platitudes do nothing to soothe and are received with anger and frustration. The cure is elusive because it too is a feeling: a feeling of connection, a place of belonging, a sense of kinship that can be as fleeting and capricious as the disease itself. Belonging that comes at odd times and in odd places and spaces, sometimes places where you least expect it and most long for it. It could be a talk with someone who knows or an evening spent with immigrants and refugees, an essay by someone who "gets" it or a visit to a restaurant where the smells and grimy floor transport you to a place of safety and belonging.

And when the cure does come, it reaches deep into the longing soul and I realize that I can take one more step, seeing beyond myself and reaching forward to what lies ahead. I am suddenly content with life on the ground. I settle back into my reality, cured for a time with hopes that the next episode will not be as acute.

Passports to Popularity

"You cut off that Levi's tag!" she screamed. "You just cut off your passport to popularity." My friend had recently entered the United States after living as a third culture kid in Europe her entire life. She had bought a pair of Levi's jeans, expensive, sleek, and svelte, like nothing she had ever worn. This was the era when Levi's were "The Jean." The era before Diesel, Guess and Lucky brands came on the scene.

But when my friend got home, she took scissors to the jeans and went for that little red tag on the butt, the one that says to the world, "I wear Levi's! I'm cool!," the tag that calls out "She belongs." My friend had just finished cutting the tag with the sharp edge of her sewing scissors when her sister screamed at her.

The words were a deep cut for a third culture kid. Depending on where you were raised, fashion (or being out of fashion) was a big deal. Many of us were away from the United States for four-year periods; things change a lot in four years. Hems go up and down, jeans go wide and narrow, florals are exchanged for plaids. Meanwhile, the oblivious third culture kid is eating curry and rice and shopping for a *shalwar-kameez*.

As third culture kids we needed our passports to popularity. Like Cady Heron, Lindsay Lohan's character in *Mean Girls*, who came from years of homeschooling in Africa, we were coming from a different land and different customs. Where we came from Levi's meant nothing and Western fashion was known only minimally. And like Cady, who made a choice to join a group of fake, disingenuous teens who focused on promoting themselves at the expense of others (The Plastics) some of us made bad choices, all for the sake of a passport to popularity. But behind the seemingly shallow and empty desire for popularity is the bigger issue of identity and belonging. Wanting to fit comfortably, boasting that we live between worlds, yet knowing we stick out like red tags on black Levi's.

There is a story, perhaps apocryphal, perhaps true, about a family that lived in a small village in Zambia. They spent years at a time at this village, going to larger cities only occasionally and to the United States, their passport country, only every four years. The mom was tired of having people know immediately on arrival in major US airports that her kids were missionary kids. If the vague, disoriented look on arrival did not shout to the world "We just came from Zambia," the clothes certainly did. They were never in fashion. She resolved that their clothes would never give away the inner turmoil of feeling displaced and "other." With that in mind, weeks before going on a home leave she had a J.C. Penney catalog delivered via slow mail. With her children she pored over the pictures of white kids with blonde hair and blue eyes in the latest fashions and, pictures in hand, they headed to a talented tailor in the big city. They arrived in the United States looking good. Almost like those kids from the catalogue. As they went through customs, the official with his U.S. immigration badge looked at the mom and smiled "So," he said, "you guys are missionaries?"

"How do you know?" she exclaimed, frustrated and bewildered. He pointed behind her and there walked her children, every last one of them with a suitcase balanced perfectly on their heads.

Apocryphal or not, I love the story. It is our story. Our story of trying, but not quite making it. A story of learning that passports to popularity are fickle, capricious, culturally relative, and overrated! While one year those passports may be a shirt from Abercrombie & Fitch, the next it could be something very different.

But the passport with stamps in it is always renewable. Even after it expires we get to keep the old one with its wide range of stamps, signifying entry into places that hold our hearts. Jeans may come and go. But passports? They remain our tickets to the world we love. Passports can never be overrated and never grow old. Can they?

The Giant Chipmunk

"Why is everyone hugging the giant chipmunk?" I asked Cliff. We were dating at the time, and it was our first visit to Disney World. For weeks, we had talked about going to Florida. It was now September, and we had dated since early January. The trip was a big one. This would be my first opportunity to meet Cliff's parents and family. And we would go to the Magic Kingdom! Disney World! Cliff had lived in Florida and had been many times. For me, it was a first.

And so we made the trip, flying into Florida just when leaves begin to change to a brilliant autumn-gold in the north, but summer remains in the south. And one day, as anticipated, we rose early and drove to Orlando to stand in line at the gates of the Magic Kingdom. It was the ideal time. Lines were short, kids were back in school, temperatures were in the high eighties, sunny, without a drop of humidity. Perfect.

Then a giant chipmunk sidled up to the crowd and people start hugging him. To say I was out of my comfort zone is a grave injustice to that zone. I was like a Martian on earth. I was Jell-O and everyone else was crème brûlée. I was fuchsia and everyone around me was blue.

When I asked Cliff to explain, he was blank-faced.

"Wait, you don't know who the chipmunk is?"

That day I learned a valuable lesson about Chip & Dale, Mickey & Minnie, Bambi & Faline, Lady & the Tramp, Dumbo and so many more. Disney had taken off on television during my childhood. My contemporaries grew up with the magic of these characters and their escapades. Kids raised in the United States knew them all. I did not. And the Magic Kingdom exposed my cultural illiteracy.

There are many more amusing examples of this cultural illiteracy. From popular TV shows to idioms, I was about five years behind pop-culture. Initially it was funny. Truth is, I am not sure when I suddenly found it a deficit. For years I laughed them off, seeing them for what they were - simply gaps based on a different upbringing. Then, suddenly, later in adulthood, my cultural illiteracy became a deficit, an insecurity, a character flaw. Is it because I was back in the U.S. raising TCK's of my own? Is it because I was suddenly uneasy in my skin, no longer able to claim I was from Pakistan or Egypt, knowing that my residency at the time included a Victorian home in an all-white town? I'm not sure. It was probably all those things and more. Perhaps I had learned, painfully, that cultural difference, long enjoyed by me, was not enjoyed by everybody. Many of my neighbors found cultural differences threatening.

In the past few years, I've begun to laugh at the gaps again, and to enjoy remembering some of the glaring errors I've made in cross-cultural living. Instead of silencing these, I find venues for stories and illustrations, places where the narratives mean something and lead toward better understanding, if not agreement. It is a step forward, as big as the giant chipmunk.

Shoplifting spells Belonging

"You're coming home with me!" the cute sixteen-year-old girl exclaimed. "We're going to have so much fun! We're going to laugh and go shopping and try on clothes and....I'm going to teach you how to shoplift." It was 1976 and we had just met in the lobby of a New England church. New England in the Seventies was not kind to difference. It didn't matter whether the difference came in the form of a visible immigrant with a strong accent and different skin tone, or as an invisible immigrant with no accent but a foreign mind-set. Different equaled abnormal. It was to New England that I would go every four years from Pakistan, my place of home and community. Though difficult, I usually succeeded in adjusting to the school setting - my differences were appealing to a certain set of people and they would take me under their wings and find me, dare I say, charming and humorous.

Church was another story. Yet church was a crucial part of a missionaries homecoming and thus part of mine.

Home to the Great Awakening in the 1700's, the New England landscape is dotted with picturesque, small churches with carefully guarded parking spots for the church organist. Only the ignorant or newcomer would dare poach that sacred spot. These small, often struggling churches had many people with hearts of kindness and interest in the world. But their children, unused to newcomers and at egocentric life stages, did not always welcome strangers, especially those from another world. I was a defiant and obstinate sixteen-year-old, and I found the effort to relate to these new peers burdensome and annoying.

The church on this particular Sunday was in Nashua, New Hampshire. We had already attended Sunday school. My twelve-year-old brother and I were standing in the lobby when the sixteen-year-old in a blue dress with cute hair and a cuter personality approached me. I was shocked, and I was thrilled. With one sentence, bizarre as it may seem, I belonged. To her I was not from another world. I was a kid! I was coming to her house, and she had things to teach me. I am not advocating shoplifting. It is wrong. It is a crime. In fact, I only recently told my parents about the incident, and I have often wondered where this girl, who I giggled with the rest of the afternoon, is spending her time.

But all that aside, this sixteen-year-old girl accepted me into her world, treated me normally, and in her acceptance of me, I became secure. We did not pay for our breath mints that day. I was petrified, and never tried to shoplift again. But petty crime was a small segment of our time together. We spent most of the afternoon talking, giggling, trying on clothes, and eating chocolate. The feelings of isolation that had begun my day were gone, in their place the warmth of belonging and illegally fresh breath.

Guest Towels

For one week after we came home from boarding school we would get to use the guest towels.

The guest towels were thick, vibrant oranges, rusts, and browns. The colors contrasted just like the material — one side velvet, the other rough. They were not like our other towels. Our other towels were worn from the hot sun of the Sindh desert. They were threadbare in spots with faded colors. Nor were they like our boarding school towels. Towels that always came home in far worse shape than when they had been packed months before in large, metal trunks, name tags sewn on their edges with tiny stitches. The guest towels were rich. They were expensive. They were special. Like us.

They were my mom's way of saying "We missed you so much! We're so glad you're home! You are special! You are our children and I really, really wish I didn't have to send you away so far and for so long."

Never mind that a week later we were back to using threadbare towels. Never mind that in a month all the sibling bickering, rivalry, teasing, and chaos would fill our house with little room for guest anything. Never mind that magic wears thin and guest towels are put back into the cupboard.

What mattered was the welcome, the warmth, the belonging. We were home. For that first week those guest towels said it all, held it all.

We would meet at the Rohri Station in Sukkur. The train would slowly chug into the station and tired, smelly bodies would jump out onto the platform. While heavy trunks and *bisters* were unloaded, we were shyly reunited as a family. We had lived apart for three months, now we were together.

On the long ride home, along bumpy roads accompanied by oxcarts and loudly painted trucks and buses, talk was sometimes slow in coming. We had to gradually get used to being together again, become accustomed to communicating in person with parents who we knew through letters. And when we got home, a favorite meal was waiting. It may be just my memory, but I think it was served on china – dishes usually reserved for guests.

And then tired bodies went to bathrooms to wash and get ready for bed and there they were welcoming us – the guest towels.

To this day I love guest towels.

My People

Their names roll off my tongue as I look across the dining room — Joanne and Suzie, Jonathan and Marg, Lynn and Debbie, Laura and Rowena and so many more. Their faces are familiar but different, their hair streaked with grey or full white, their gait is not as strong as I remember, their eyes are dimming.

I am at a reunion of people who share my past and my faith. These are my people.

Lake Michigan lies in the background, as vast as an ocean. As vast as the time and experiences that have passed since I have seen these people. For some it has been forty years, for others it has been three but it doesn't matter. Conversation comes quickly and without restraint, both memories and present day life shared.

I don't have to explain house parents or train rides or first days in boarding school. They too grew up in the shadow of mosques, hearing the call to prayer, smelling spices from the bazaar and fresh mangoes from the trees. We have all come here because we share the experience that is growing up in Pakistan, and the nomadic life of a third culture kid.

A couple of years ago while living in Arizona I was asked to speak at a meeting for native tribes at Navajo nation. It was a small meeting and we began with a blessing and introductions. The introductions didn't include job – that was unimportant. They included tribe, father and mesa – this was their tribe. I watched and listened, every person secure in who they were in their tribe, their family, their mesa.

And then it came to me. And I don't have a tribe. I was paralyzed. So I admitted it. "I don't have a tribe. So I have to tell you what my job is – I'm so sorry!" They were gracious and lovely in their acceptance, but I felt this lack of belonging. As silly as it sounds, I wanted a tribe.

Today. Today I am with my tribe, my people. These are my people. They know who my father is, who my mother is, who my brothers are, where I went to school. There is little I have to explain for these are my people and I belong.

Belonging

We all know what it feels like. The stomach-knotting knowledge that we weren't invited, that we don't belong. Our first memories of being left out usually come early in life and can be as simple as not being invited to a birthday party or as complicated as becoming a part of a blended family, where suddenly we realize the family we thought we belonged to no longer exists.

Just as a yellow police line blocks off a crime scene, only allowing those with authority inside, there is a line and we are not allowed inside that line.

Belonging. Just saying the word can cause pain in many. What is belonging in all its complexity? What is belonging when you are of a third culture? If you live between worlds, do you belong in no man's land — that strange, twilight space of 'not there yet'? What if you are considered 'half' like 'half' asian or 'half' black? Do you belong to one half or the other? Are you half of a whole? Will you ever be considered more than half?

In *The Weight of Glory,* in a chapter based on a lecture called *The Inner Ring,* C.S. Lewis takes a profound look at belonging, specifically at our desire to belong.

I believe that in all men's lives at certain periods, and in many men's lives at all periods between infancy and extreme old age, one of the most dominant elements is the desire to be inside the local Ring and the terror of being left outside.

The Inner Ring is that elusive place of belonging that is just beyond our reach, just past our grasp. Because once we have reached that inner ring and we begin to settle, we think we've finally found a place to belong, until we realize there is a ring beyond that — and once we've gotten to that ring, there's a ring beyond that still.

In elementary school that inner ring is the group of girls that excludes us. They are a part of Something Special and we don't belong. It's that group in middle school that get together every Friday night and we're not invited, that group in high school that bears the name and reputation 'cool' and we do not know cool, no matter how hard we try. And though we'd like it to stop there, it often continues. Its college, then as a young adult, then work and getting into that inner, secure, exclusive place. Its church and those people who are in that inner circle, the circle that seems so Godly and confident, the one that we wish we belonged to. And yet when we get close, there's something beyond, just out of our grasp.

We constantly look to that place of belonging that seems so secure, that tells us we have 'arrived, yet it continually eludes us.

This has been a deep struggle at different periods in my life. At times I have faced tremendous insecurity around 'belonging.' I have had times when I have desperately tried to get to that inner ring, that place where I fully belong, where there are no voices telling me I'm not really a part of the group. I've had other times where I think I have arrived at that inner place of belonging only to realize there is something missing — there's another ring to pass through.

This inner ring can be in any area of life…whether it's around nationality, academics, status, or church. We are not born understanding these rings or how to get into them.

At the beginning of the essay, Lewis poses this question:

> I will ask only one question—and it is, of course, a rhetorical question which expects no answer. In the whole of your life as you now remember it, has the desire to be on the right side of that invisible line ever prompted you to any act or word on which, in the cold small hours of a wakeful night, you can look back with satisfaction? If so, your case is more fortunate than most.

To be a part of that inner ring often means acting or speaking in ways that we end up regretting, we forget who we are, we lose our way, all in the quest to get to the inner ring. Sometimes getting to the inner ring involves giving up our integrity, and pretending we are someone who we aren't.

Lewis' response to this dilemma of the "Inner Ring" is to break the cycle. "The quest of the Inner Ring will break your hearts unless you break it." If we break this cycle, we will find ourselves still perhaps on the outside, but no longer will this be a burden, no longer will we wear ourselves out by trying so hard to make it inside. Instead we will find our place, sometimes in the most unlikely of circles.

Counterintuitive as it seems, this has been my story. When I finally stopped grasping at success, at confidence, at belonging, I inexplicably found it. It is hard to articulate , even more difficult on paper. All I know is that somehow the quest that felt like a burden on my back since boarding school days of popular groups and cliques, has slowly but steadily been broken. In some mysterious way, I belong.

All of this is reminiscent to me of the words in the Gospel of Matthew: "Whoever finds their life will lose it, and whoever loses their life for my sake will find it." Indeed C.S. Lewis speaks to this as well:

> "If we find ourselves with a desire that nothing in this world can satisfy, the most probable explanation is that we were made for another world."

Airports

Being able to travel is one of life's greatest gifts. It simultaneously keeps one humble and fully alive. And for me the gift and magic begin at the airport. The airport is a place where I don't have to try. It's where I can be fully comfortable between worlds.

Arrival

*L*ove Actually begins with a scene like the one in which I am now a part. Unabashed hugging between friends or lovers; tears on the faces of sisters and parents; repeated kissing on each side of the cheek depending on cultural background.

I remember the opening lines from the movie as I wait at the arrival area of Terminal E in Boston's Logan Airport:

> *Whenever I get gloomy with the state of the world, I think about the arrivals gate at Heathrow Airport. General opinion's starting to make out that we live in a world of hatred and greed, but I don't see that. It seems to me that love is everywhere. Often it's not particularly dignified or newsworthy, but it's always there - fathers and sons, mothers and daughters, husbands and wives, boyfriends, girlfriends, old friends. When the planes hit the Twin Towers, as far as I know none of the phone calls from the people on board were messages of hate or revenge - they were all messages of love.*

I had a friend tell me that he had never experienced anything like the reuniting of a third culture kid and his family at the Islamabad Airport in Pakistan. He was overwhelmed with the emotion shown in those moments of arrival.

An arrival is the end of one journey, the beginning of another. You can feel the emotions all around you. Longing, excitement, nervous anticipation, a bit of fear, the slightly dry mouth, and frequent swallowing. They are loudly unspoken. The watchers are oblivious to those not in their party. All eyes are on the large double doors that come from Immigration and Baggage Claim.

Each time the doors open I watch everyone in the room strain to see. Is it the one they love? Is it the one they have waited for? The girls with the balloons step up and hold out their welcome sign, they are noisy in their excitement, giving bear hugs to the arrivals. The rest of us relax for a moment - it's not yet our turn.

Arrival. It is so hard to explain those thoughts and feelings. But when we see those scenes in movies, we know exactly what it feels like.

I hear many languages around me: Spanish, Russian, Arabic, Hindi, English, German. Though the languages differ, the tone of anticipation sounds similar. The area is crowded. Three international flights, from Germany, Iceland and Mexico, have arrived at the same time.

Distracted, we can't get into deep conversations. Instead, we're in our own worlds and thoughts, we are this close to tasting reunion, and it is so sweet. So much has happened since loved ones left – new babies and jobs, illness and conflict, bad storms and sunshine. Most of all there has been daily life that had to readjust to the absence of the ones who left, daily life minus extra spots at dinner tables and extra voices in conversations.

When they left we worried about overweight suitcases

and going above luggage allowances, communicating during emergencies and making sure passports were current. When they left, we felt it was forever. When they left, our pillows held our tears.

But when they left is far away from where we now stand. The leaving was from another time. Now? Now we stand with comradely understanding of those waiting with us. It's all a part of Arrival. And it makes the leaving all worthwhile.

Field Trip to the Airport

Last night I flew out of Logan Airport in Boston, boarding a plane to Seattle. Despite the late night arrival, this morning I've woken up to the bliss of the unfamiliar and the sense of all things new in a different city. Not least I am enjoying a luxurious king size bed with multiple pillows and a state-of-the-art television.

Like many third culture kids, I find myself drawn to airports. From the anticipation of the ticket purchase, through the multiple details of packing and preparing, to the stripping down assault on my person during the pre-departure security process and the happy tiredness of arrival, the airport has played a prominent and satisfying role in my life.

When my daughter Stefanie was in kindergarten, her teacher arranged for the class to take a field trip to Logan Airport in Boston. The children were extremely excited. They would be given fake tickets, get on a real plane, see how the luggage got from person to plane and back, eat a meal, and experience a behind the scenes look at an airport.

It was one of the hardest days of my second year in the United States. As we drove up to the airport, twenty four kids with backpacks and bows in hair, and parents who somehow managed to rearrange schedules to be on the trip, were chatting happily. And lost amidst the chatter was a third culture kid whose identity was in crisis.

A field trip to the airport? No! I belonged on the departing plane. We were the family for whom airports were a passage to another home. We were the family to whom people waved goodbye. The family of a kindergartener who went on a field trip to the airport? That we were not.

Except that we were. We no longer lived in Pakistan or Egypt. We had a legal address in a small town in New England. We held documented proof of residence from the Commonwealth of Massachusetts in the form of drivers' licenses. We no longer had the overseas address and everything that accompanied it.

What happens when the third culture kid becomes an adult and settles in their passport country? For a time everything seems backwards and contrary. Few of us had the dreams of owning our own homes, or becoming "successful" as defined by middle-class America. Our parents had lived counter-culture and had passed that on to us. Nothing really prepared us for a life in suburbs or small towns of the Western hemisphere.

So the challenge is to transfer all that enables us to live well cross-culturally and apply it to living in our passport countries. It's about finding the kindred spirits that we need during the rocky points. It's about learning to forget about ourselves... that's the hardest part. The part of growing up enough to live beyond my feelings and discomfort, using my sense of being "other" as a bridge to work with the marginalized and uncomfortable in my community.

Field trips to airports are not for me, and I continue to long to get on planes when I head to the airport. These days I am vicariously living through my children as I pick them up from one country or another. I've come to realize that longing is ok as long as it does not paralyze, as long as I slowly continue to embrace the life that has been given at this time, at this moment.

Right now, it's easy for me to be content. After all, I took a six-hour plane trip across the country last night. Even though I am not flying internationally, I'm not on a field trip. I'm on a real trip with a real plane and all that comes with it. It's during the days following a trip that I need grace to live fully. Until then, I will enjoy this moment.

The Passenger in 17D

I boarded the plane with a sigh of exhaustion. It had been a busy day and trying to complete everything that I needed to, as well as prepare for the trip I was now embarking on, had seemed impossible. And then finally Zone Three was called and I could go and relax for the three-hour plane ride. Nothing would be expected of me during those three hours that I was high in the sky, above the height of Mount Everest. I would be able to do whatever I chose. And what I was going to choose was sleep.

As I moved into 17E by the window, 17D looked at me and smiled. He was a nice businessman of indeterminate age. "Good," I thought. "No talking. He won't want to talk to me, and I won't want to talk to him. This is so perfect!" But my inner conversation with myself was interrupted by 17D. "Going home?" he asked. "No, just a quick overnight trip for work," I replied. Pause. "How about you?" I finally said. And the conversation began. Within seconds came the dreaded "Where are you from?" Paralysis followed by panic. Suddenly I am a little kid again. Am I from where I am currently living? Am I from where I grew up? Am I from my birthplace? The options are many, the feelings are overwhelming.

I looked at 17D. "That's a hard question." I proceeded to give him as little information as possible. He grasped it. He was from Denmark and had come to the United States ten years ago, uprooting his entire family for what he thought would be two years. His children are third culture kids, coping with a life between the worlds of Denmark and the United States. We talked for a good hour and I forgot my tiredness, forgot my desire to sit back and rest. We talked about Europe and the Middle East, Pakistan and Afghanistan, Atlanta and Boston.

We talked about spouses and kids. We talked about raising kids between countries and the wonder, but sometimes schizophrenia that resulted. And finally, we talked about faith — faith as paramount to our existence, faith as the guiding force in our lives. Far from making me more tired, I was in awe. In awe that thirty seven thousand feet in the air a total stranger and I had so much in common and had finally come around to talking about that which was most important to both of us.

We talked about trust. How hard it was at times to trust God with our lives, our jobs, and our kids. And then in a thirty seven thousand foot epiphany I thought about how at that moment, and from the beginning of the trip, we were putting our trust in a pilot and an airline industry that we didn't know. We trusted a pilot to get us from point A to point B without another thought. We didn't know if he'd been drinking or was exhausted from lack of sleep. We didn't know if reliable mechanics or people who took short cuts had serviced the plane. But we trusted this human being, this fallible industry, with our lives.

And I sometimes wonder if God, the Sovereign God, the God who does not grow weary, whose strength none of us can fathom, is trustworthy? Within this epiphany was a loving rebuke.

Our trip ended. We exchanged cards. I invited him for dinner with us next time he is in Boston. He told me about a great book he was reading. In sleepy awe, I headed toward baggage claim, my mind and heart full of epiphanies and the passenger in 17D.

I Flew Before I Walked

"We would like to travel," said the young woman wistfully as she patted the head of her eighteen month old. I waited for the "But." I knew it was coming. She didn't disappoint. "But he's too young. Besides with a child it just wouldn't work." I bit my tongue until I could taste blood. "Oh" I said calmly, and the angel on my right side told me "Be empathetic!" The devil on my left said, "Tell her she's CRAZY!" So I just said "Oh!" again.

This was not the first time I had heard this from a mom or a dad. I once talked to a man who worked for an airline. The entire family could fly free. Anywhere. "Too much work," he said in a matter of fact way to my husband. "Besides, they won't appreciate it!" "Oh? And a thirteen year old will?" I thought, holding my tongue.

These conversations make me crazy. Too young? Too much work? There is no too young to travel. If you don't start kids on the road or plane when they are young then too soon they, and you, will move into a place and state of mind that sees all the obstacles instead of the benefits. The obstacle of the toddler who seems to need more luggage than the rest of the family combined — certainly more than the family from

The Sudan who can fit all their possessions into two bags. The obstacles of a house that needs updating, jobs that consume our lives, and kids unwilling to try anything new.

When teenage taste buds, used to familiar foods, are unwilling to try the foreign, when lack of flexibility is apparent to all, so used are they to traveling in comfort from your house to grandma's, when they are in their most egocentric phase of life – that's when many people begin to travel with their kids. It doesn't make sense.

I flew before I walked. At three months of age I was packed up, along with diapers and dollies, and taken on a journey across the ocean in a ship called the Julius Caesar. We left from New York City harbor. One of my favorite pictures is of my mom, a young woman with lovely short, dark, curls, outfit complete with gloves and pearls, holding me on the deck of the ship.

I flew before I walked. Perhaps that accounts for my love of airports and airplanes, my love of all things related to travel. I was irrationally jealous of the suitcase I bought for my daughter before she left for Italy. With various sizes and shapes of pockets, it was nicer than any I have ever had. I am addicted to websites advertising airline deals.

I flew before I walked. I feel rooted everywhere, and nowhere. I will sit down with fellow immigrants and feel an immediate connection even if we have no verbal means to communicate. But with my fellow English speakers, I often feel like I face un-crossable boundaries.

I remind myself, when I feel restless and my feet feel too pinned to the ground, that I flew before I walked. And now, it seems inevitable, I have kids who flew before they walked.

Airport Eyes

Four-fifteen am alarm ringing. Bleary morning eyes. Slightly snappy but excited interactions. Fumbling to find my ID and the boarding pass that I had so carefully printed yesterday. Finally relaxing at Gate thirty one, watching a sunrise over the Atlantic Ocean through the windows of Terminal C. I have Airport Eyes as I gaze across at people, looking but not seeing, in my world of possibility and promise.

Only two nights before we waited at Logan's International Terminal for Annie, our daughter, to arrive from Cairo for our son's wedding. My airport eyes watched the unembarrassed, open emotion of arriving travelers greeting family members and friends with hugs, laughter, and tear. One family expressed their joy through handshakes; another placed numerous kisses on both sides of the cheeks of no less than ten family members. Through airport eyes, I wondered what had transpired in their lives since they last saw each other. So much had happened since we last said our goodbyes at the beginning of 2011. Annie had been a frontline witness to the January twenty fifth uprising in Egypt, and had learned how to distinguish live ammunition from empty shells.

Third culture kids may be more loyal to an airline than a country. For some of us, frequent flyer balances are more important than savings accounts. At airports, life seems full of endless possibilities. Whether I am traveling to Rochester, New York or Karachi, I enter the terminal and get airport eyes, seeing the world through the lens of hope and opportunity.

Bridges to the World

In the daze that comes with early morning travel, we dropped off our rental car and began winding our way through the confusing maze of the terminal, making our mandated stops at check-in, security, and coffee shop.

The airport was already alive with activity. I walked through the various stops, mesmerized by the myriads of people and worlds connecting. As so often happens, when I am at this home away from home called the airport, I was lost in amazement. In this place and space worlds were connecting.

If a bridge is a structure that connects two points or places together, then airports are our bridges to the world.

Families from China, Peru, Colombia, and Germany, businessmen and women, students returning from college, and men and women dressed in military uniform mingle together, all going somewhere, all leaving this space for another world.

If airports are the bridges, people do the bridge building. You can pass through hundreds of airports in a lifetime never leaving the airport, never understanding the city, country and people who live beyond its walls and runway fences. The bridge loses its efficacy. Whether the city be Delhi or Mumbai;

Dubai or Frankfurt; Karachi or São Paulo, the airport is just a tool for the bridge builder. It can't serve as the human connection that is so critical in building understanding.

Building bridges means moving beyond my enclave of cultural comfort, moving to a place of cultural humility and willingness to learn. As I sleepily drink my gourmet coffee with the shot of hazelnut and the two squirts of cream, hurriedly purchased from a shop crowded with fellow travelers, I appreciate being on this bridge between worlds. On this bridge, I don't have to think too hard about either the place I've been or the place where I'm going. It's a resting place before the bridge building.

The bridge building will come later today as I once again reconcile my personality with the reserve that often characterizes the place where I unpack my suitcase and hang my heart.

Mumbai Airport

It's 2am in the Mumbai Airport. I am in the domestic terminal and the airport is quiet. Outside the sky is dark and the open doors reveal small restaurants, some closed, others open with minimal food and one lone employee to serve customers who happen by at that hour. We arrived here at midnight. It's still three hours before our flight to Goa. We don't yet know that we will miss that flight.

At the door the guard's sleepy eyes belie his quick response. Some people in our group have already tested his reflexes. His high turban is immaculate, and a thick silver Sikh bracelet falls heavy on his arm.

Other passengers are scattered in the two seating areas, either in semi-sleep or randomly observing their surroundings with the resigned expressions of travelers in transit, travelers who are between worlds, in the limbo of the 'not yet arrived.'

A group from the Emirates walks across the terminal, a gaggle of children lagging behind, weary with the weight traveling and the weight of bags, hanging heavy off their backs, luggage tags bearing the characteristic red and white emblem of the airline. Their moms are ahead of them, slender and tall in abayas, only their eyes showing through black *niqabs*.

I sit back and look around. This waiting in terminals is a world I know well. I've never counted up the hours I have spent like this, just waiting, but they are many.

It's amazing how much waiting there is in a life of movement. Surrounded by luggage, tired from crossing time zones, we just sit. We wait. We wait in transit, in the in-between, not always sure of the next piece of the journey. We wait for buses. We wait at train stations. We wait at airports.

And there's another kind of waiting. We wait for visas, that legal stamp of permission to enter a country as a guest or live there as a resident. We wait for donors to fund projects. We wait for decisions over which we have no control. We wait for a doctor's approval to continue this life overseas.

Above all, we wait for God. We move forward in faith, only to be stopped in transit. So we wait. It's not time. We sit tight. There are dozens of ways that God moves in and orchestrates our plans, our movements. We may never know the reason for the waiting. It may elude us until the day we die and we're on the other side of eternity.

For waiting is nothing new to the work of God. In waiting we join hundreds of others who waited before us. Joseph, sold into slavery, waited years to be able to say the words "You meant it to harm me, but God used it for good…" Abraham and Sarah, waited for so many years to have a child that Sarah laughed cynically at the idea. Noah waited aboard a boat full of antsy animals, with no land in sight. Those are only a few in a long list of 'waiters'

And so I wait at two am in the Mumbai airport, thinking of this God who reaches through time and place and asks us to be okay in the in-between, to trust his character and his love. Giving thanks to a God who is utterly trustworthy and completely unpredictable, a God who knows all about waiting as he daily waits for his children to finally get it.

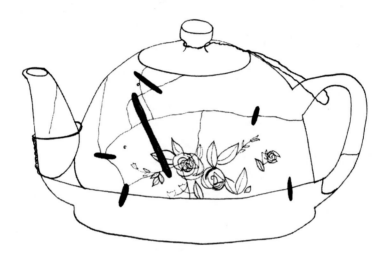

Grief & Loss

I know where to take this ache, but it feels heavy and I'm not sure I can carry it and drop it at those feet, those dust-covered, blistered, scarred feet of Jesus.

Saudade

I have heard it described as a unique word with no equivalent in English. Originally Portuguese, the word was first used in the thirteenth century. It describes a longing, a melancholy, a desire for what was. It is *saudade*.

Immigrants and refugees search for words that adequately describe the peculiar longing for what they left behind – not the war and evil that is a relief to escape, but the land, the people, the food and all that evokes home. Doctors and nurses working with large populations of immigrants and refugees often simply put it down as "depression."

A health center I know desperately tried to find out through a survey what percentage of their immigrant and refugee patients had depression. The survey was unsuccessful. It did not reflect the narrative that these health care providers were hearing from patients.

One day a woman from Haiti said to them "Have you ever thought about asking patients if they are homesick." They looked at her in surprise. No, they had not. With a simple change of a word, they felt they were more able to get to the heart of the feeling. But is it depression? Depression is defined as a "Severe despondency and dejection, accompanied by feelings of hopelessness and inadequacy." That is not what immigrants are describing.

What they describe are feelings so deep that you can scarcely give words to them. Your throat catches. You experience an intense, but wordless, longing and desire. How do I know this? Because I have experienced it, first hand. What we long to describe is *Saudade*.

> *The famous* saudade *of the Portuguese is a vague and constant desire for something that does not and probably cannot exist, for something other than the present, a turning towards the past or towards the future; not an active discontent or poignant sadness but an indolent dreaming wistfulness.* A. F. G. Bell *In Portugal of 1912*

Many know that they will never go back to the place where they feel most at home. They realistically accept this, but not without *saudade*. A Portuguese friend of mine recently told me about her father. He is in his nineties and came to the United States with a large family over fifty years ago. A year ago, he went back to Portugal for what everyone thought would be a short trip. Now over a year later, he is still there. All the years he was in the United States, he experienced *saudade*. He has returned so he no longer has to experience this intense longing; he is back in a place where he is viscerally at home, in a land that he loves.

Third culture kids often struggle to give voice to their longing. Well aware that they are not from the country or countries where they were raised, they still have all the connections and feelings that represent home. When trying to voice these, others look on with glazed eyes. Just recently, someone said to me "But you're not an immigrant! You're American!" The tone was accusing. It was meant to be. What was unsaid was "Give it a rest! We know you grew up overseas. Big deal. You're American and you're living in America."

Ah, yes…but I have *saudade*. I have that longing for something that "does not and cannot exist." I know that it cannot be. And on my good days, it is well hidden under the culture and costume of which I am now living. But on my more difficult days, it struggles to find voice only to find that explaining is too difficult.

Finding the word gives voice to these longings. I have often been looked at with impatience "Third culture kids are not that different!" says the skeptic. "We all have times of longing" but I would argue, gently, that our experience is different. We are neither of one world nor the other, but between. Our earliest memories are shaped by sights, sounds, and smells that we now experience only in brief travels or through movies and television. All of those physical elements that shaped our early forays into this world are of another world. And so we experience *saudade*. And the simple discovery of a word gives meaning to those feelings, and can validate and heal.

Pivotal Journeys

I thought my world had ended. Only moments before I had been in the Islamabad International Airport terminal saying a tearful goodbye to my high school boyfriend. Now, as I stepped from the hot tarmac into the waiting Pakistan International Airways plane, I was leaving – forever it seemed to me – the country that had been home to me since I was three months old.

It was 1978. I had just graduated from high school in Pakistan. The night before was a blur of celebration. Pomp and Circumstance accompanied ten of us on our slow procession down the aisle of the old stone church building that served as our main school auditorium. Wearing bright blue gowns and caps, tassels proudly proclaiming a brass '78, we walked confidently to the stage. Piano and voice performances were followed by valedictory speeches enthusiastically applauded by our large, sometimes loud, occasionally nosy, always interested, mission family. A reception followed the graduation ceremony and homemade goodies mixed with punch, hugs, and goodbyes. Graduation was the event of the summer. This was our time. We had watched many other classes experience this rite of passage, this honor. Now it was our turn.

The evening had been a highlight of my short time on this earth, but the morning after had not gone smoothly. My parents and I had one of our not-so-shining moments arguing over what I should wear on the plane.

Pakistan was then, as now, a conservative Muslim country, and I (although I would now argue otherwise) was a Western teenager. I had opted to wear jeans and a short top, the fashion of the year.

"No, No, No" my mother said in her I Mean Business voice. "We still live in Pakistan and you cannot wear that outfit!"

She was adamant – and correct. But I was eighteen. The bitter fight that followed was not pretty. My tongue ran away with my mouth until a stern rebuke from my father reconnected my brain to my words.

The van that was to pick us up and take us the two hours down the mountain to the airport soon arrived, and my parents and I were forced into an unhappy truce. For my part, I suspended hostilities because the Boyfriend and his Father were in the car.

As I boarded the plane I knew that life as I had known it – the life of boarding school and long train trips home, friends and surrogate aunties and uncles, curry, *chapattis* and chai in Jhika Gali on weekend evenings – was ending. And with that knowledge came deep feelings of loss and grief. The feelings were left unspoken because of the trauma of the day, but they were there nevertheless, and I would remember them for years to come. I was one plane ride away from losing family, identity, and skills that had proved themselves so necessary and reliable during my formative years.

An unspoken question was lurking in my mind. I did not dare voice it, but it was loud and overwhelming. Could the God who had sustained me through my early years – through a broken wrist from playing Steal the Bacon on the small court outside the front of the school building, through homesickness, car accidents, and so much more – sustain me through this new journey? Did He actually live in America? Foolish as that may sound, this was the resounding cry of my heart.

The plane's engines roared and the plane took off. The pretty Pakistani airline hostess in green and white *shalwar Kameez*, *dupatta* draped gracefully over her head, gave emergency instructions and we were off to Karachi on the first leg of our journey.

This story, like all my stories, is told through my perception and is limited by my perspective. But there were also other stories and other perspectives that day. This is what my mother recalls:

"Honestly I don't have a clear memory of that particular disagreement with you, but it's probably pretty much as you remember it. Graduation the night before had been such a wonderful time, a real high point. And now we had to go. What I do remember is feeling torn up that this day had come – you, our little girl graduated from MCS and going off on your own. How could we abandon you to the big bad Western world and come back to Pakistan?... I remember taking a last walk through Forest Dell as the van waited at the top of the path. I wasn't checking to see if we had forgotten anything. We wouldn't be living there again. It was pretty near the end of our summers as they had been for all our time in Pakistan.

And I felt completely undone inside. I could see our life ahead with no kids with us, and I didn't know if I could do it."

My dad had this short but poignant perspective: "I really don't remember the fight or the flight to Karachi. I do remember seeing our only daughter walk down the ramp in Heathrow Airport to go to Scotland by herself. And I am sure we prayed hard! You didn't look back or wave goodbye, and you looked very brave and independent."

This was the beginning of a new step for all of us. Behind every third culture kid is a parent – a parent who wishes, hopes, and prays that they are doing the right thing.

Grieving Well

Those of us who have grown up as third culture kids accumulate layer upon layer of loss. According to Dave Pollock, a man who did more to understand the third culture kid experience than any other,

> One of the major areas in working with TCKs is that of . . . dealing with the issue of unresolved grief. They are always leaving or being left. Relationships are short-lived. At the end of each school year, a certain number of the student body leaves, not just for the summer, but for good. It has to be up to the parent to provide a framework of support and careful understanding as the child learns to deal with this repetitive grief. Most TCKs go through more grief experiences by the time they are 20 than monocultural individuals do in a lifetime.

We are told we need to grieve our losses. We are told that this is healthy, that this will help us move forward in life, not paralyzed by what was, instead purposeful in what now is. But what does grieving those losses look like? How do we grieve?

It strikes me, as I think about grieving and how to grieve

well, that it's something we have to learn. But how do we learn it? It helps to read books, like C.S. Lewis' *A Grief Observed* or other books in which wise writers have penned sound advice. But outside resources only go so far. In the end we must put one foot in front of the other and own our grief.

This grief and loss road has been a long one for me. It's not just about being a third culture kid. This road has been full of what it looks like to not grieve well and that's not pretty. But through the journey, I think I'm learning more of what it means to grieve well.

Here is what I've learned about grieving well.

Grief is good. You can't grieve well if you don't grieve. I grieved because I loved my life in Pakistan and then in Egypt. I loved my friendships and community, hot chai in a tea shop and shopping in Murree or Shikarpur bazaar; long afternoons during school vacations and weeks at a Karachi beach. I loved these things. My grieving is not bad. It is a protective emotion. It is cathartic. It reminds me how much I loved. Grief and grieving is a good thing. Understanding grief as something good is a first step in grieving well.

Grief is individual. It is unique. Though grief itself is universal, my response to my specific circumstance is unique. My parents and I each had our own, unique response to my graduation and leaving Pakistan on my own. My grief is caused by, and directed at, an event or series of events that are from my perspective, just as my parents grief is defined by their perspective on the same event. Just as the stamp of my fingerprint is like no other, so is my grief. Grieving well means understanding and living with the paradox of grief being universal and grief being personal and unique.

Understanding that grief is universal helps me to let others in; understanding that my grief is unique helps me to give grace when their suggestions may fall short.

Grief is rarely nicely organized. Grief doesn't fit into neat categories. Those that try to put it there rush to medicate us too quickly instead of allowing us to process, to go the hard route of finding the underlying cause of grief and slowly healing. Grieving well means understanding that it is not well-organized and the more I can accept that, the less surprised I will be when it comes on like a tsunami in the most unlikely places.

Grief is physical and emotional. Grief is exhausting. The yawning. The anger. The wanting to cry but knowing you can't. All of this is physically exhausting. Grieving well means that I'll be conscious of how grief affects me physically and do what I can to sleep and to eat well. Protein and vitamin C, those physical healers need to abound in my diet.

Grief is culturally based. From wailing at funerals in Pakistan to the stoicism in a German woman diagnosed with cancer, responses to grief are culturally formed. I cannot assume that others are not grieving because their grief 'looks' different. Grief knows no national boundaries, but it is definitely culturally bound. Grieving well means understanding how the culture where I am now living both defines and copes with grief, yet understanding that as one who knows what it is to live between worlds, I can choose to define and cope in other ways.

Laughter in the midst of grief is okay. Grieving well means understanding that laughter and joy are holy gifts.

In the midst of grief, it can be amazing to laugh until you begin to cry. It feels wrong at times. How can we laugh when something so terrible has happened, or when grief rips our souls, when we're still full of pain? The amazing truth is that we can laugh. And laughter is good. It is holy.

Spiritual truths that we believed when we weren't grieving are still true. They just don't feel true. God doesn't waste pain. Never. Part of me doesn't want to say this because it has become clichéd. But it's also truth. He doesn't waste pain. He doesn't waste grief. Period. Full stop.

He meets us under whirring fans or beside oceans, in cold bedrooms or curled up on couches. He is as present at six as he will be at sixty. He speaks to us in our grief and in our pain. And he never, ever gives up on us, even when we give up on ourselves.

The Ache

I shouldn't have gone to the job website. I knew in my heart that it would have repercussions. And it did.

I found a job posting in the Middle East. Just like that, the ache was back. The ache to live overseas again. The ache to land in an airplane on foreign soil. The ache to wake up to a language that is at once familiar and elusive. The ache to walk out on the street and greet the doorman with a smile and a *"Sabah al-khayr."* The ache to hear his *"Sabah al-noor!"* in response. The ache for open markets and smoky coffee houses. The ache of the call to prayer, its cacophony echoing across the dusty sky. The ache for smells and sounds and tastes unavailable in my current reality.

I ask for the millionth time why it won't just go away, this ache, this longing. Others I know have adjusted. They are fine with their occasional trips overseas. Others I know seem to have church communities that support them, families that surround them, and picture books that chronicle their journeys. But most of those others were born and raised here, in the United States. Their journeys to other worlds were just that, journeys to places where homesickness meant missing the United States.

I have to get on with it. I have tasks calling, deadlines chanting, and people asking. I don't have the luxury of remaining in my ache. If I do, there will be consequences. So I breathe heavily and send off a quick email to Robynn. She will understand this ache, this deep longing, this *saudade*. "I miss living overseas so much today that I hurt all over. I know you get this. Why, oh why, can't this go away? So many people I know are happy just doing their trips abroad. Why can't I be like that?"

My friend responds:

> *I do SO GET IT - I know the ache. I know the longing…for me it's like a taste…It comes up like a sweet taste and sits in my spirit like bile. I don't understand… God is all about uprooting people. He's all about the Great Commission…sending, foreign exchange, holy transfers… and we are so wired for it. We know how to do it. It comes naturally for us.… why, oh why, doesn't He see it that way? And I miss that other Robynn…the one that comes alive in Asia…the one that banters and barters, the one that is uninhibited… the Market place / Bazaar street smart Robynn. Here she is dormant. Asleep. And lately, I fear, she is dead. I grieve for her. I really liked her. We got along well.*

And in her reply I know there is understanding; there are others like me, others who ache for a place and who they are in that place.

I don't need lectures on blooming, or planting, or living well right where I am. Because, frankly, I know the lectures by heart. And I live them. No one around me would ever guess the turmoil of this inner ache. When the ache comes to the surface, those lectures are like vinegar to a wound. The empathy a fellow third culture kid gives is enough. Robynn does not admonish me, instruct me on what I should do. She sits with me and shares my heart.

I know where to take this ache, but it feels heavy. I'm not sure I can carry it and drop it at those feet, those dust-covered, blistered, scarred feet of Jesus.

I whisper words that seemed ruined when they were strategically crafted into a bestseller, but I whisper them anyway because they are real to me. They are the words of Jabez, cried from an aching heart: "Oh that you would bless me and enlarge my territory! Let your hand be with me, and keep me from harm so that I will be free from pain." (1 Chronicles 4:10)

And God granted his request.

When Grief Surfaces

Several years ago, we sold a house in Phoenix. It was a track home, nothing special, tan with desert rose trim, at the end of a cul-de-sac in a middle-income neighborhood. It was one of hundreds in the neighborhood.

But this house had a back yard, and it was the backyard that attracted us, and the backyard that we decided to develop.

In the corner where we daily viewed amazing, desert sunsets we built a patio and fireplace, sectioned off from the rest of the yard with an archway and wall. Built-in benches faced the fireplace on both sides, with a jacuzzi to the right. It was a haven. Sitting in our yard, I experienced deep peace, and also inexplicable longings.

Then we decided to sell the home, to move closer to the neighborhood high school.

Only after we had moved did I realize how much I would miss this house. Years of grief, far more grief than our few years in that house could explain, emerged from the cave to which I had banished them. Like a long-trapped creature, my grief surfaced angrily. The grief and loss were indescribable. It didn't make sense. Why had they waited so long? Why had they been dormant only to awake at such an inopportune time? Why this move and not others? Why had all of this surfaced from the selling of a track-home?

We were still completing repairs on the old house, and I would sit in the nearly empty living room, and I would grieve. The overhead ceiling fan whirred above me. The amiable workmen chatted and hammered below. And I grieved.

I grieved leaving home and going to boarding for the first time. I grieved saying goodbye to best friends. I grieved the end of first love, a childhood grief made more poignant by the unresolved grief before. I grieved leaving Pakistan, with an ache in my throat and stomach, with tears caught in that place where they can't be released. I grieved leaving Egypt, my 'adult love.' And added to that grief, I grieved the loss of the Middle East studies program my husband had sweated blood to begin. I grieved the realization that I may never live overseas again, an ache in my bones.

And in that house in Phoenix, that nothing-special-track-home with its beautiful yard, all these griefs flowed together, wave upon wave, memory upon memory, feeling upon feeling, stirred up and churned up like a dust storm that must run its course. And when the storm has passed, dust leaves behind its grit and its taste on every surface.

I don't know why it surfaced at that time in that way. It seemed to make no sense. Perhaps I was allowing myself to grieve in a way that I had previously been unable. I'll never know.

I stopped trying to analyze. I let the grief flow. Like allowing nausea to run its course without interference from pills and cures, I found that with the grief came comfort.

No human caught my tears. No flesh and blood comforted me, only God, in the sounds of a whirring fan and in words committed to memory so many years before.

Oh my God you search and you know me,
you know when I sit, you know where I rise;
you perceive my thoughts from afar...
My frame was not hidden from you when I was made in the secret place,
when I was woven together in the depths of the earth.
Your eyes saw my unformed body;
all the days ordained for me were written in your book
before one of them came to be. (Psalms 139)

Then the work was over. The house sold. It belonged to someone else. Too soon, I thought. I had more griefs to name, more sadness to resolve.

According to the conventional wisdom third culture kids suffer from unresolved grief. Hidden grief, the experts say, is a significant struggle for us. I don't know. I have done no research. I only have my own experience. But I did find, alone in an empty track home, solace in naming my grief, and comfort in verses that had rooted their way into my heart. And God, whispering comfort in the sound of a whirring fan, met me.

Community, Connection & Loneliness

I grew up with an extraordinary sense of community. First, there was a mission "family" that developed amongst my parents' colleagues in southern Pakistan. These were our surrogate aunts and uncles, functioning in place of the real aunts and uncles who were miles away and known primarily through photographs. We spent Christmases together and vacations together. Our parents felt the ache of distance from blood relatives, but as children we were perfectly content with this version of family.

A second community was shaped in boarding school. For some of us, the years of boarding school evoke strong negative emotion and unresolved pain. But my own memories are surely laced with grace. I look back and laugh, remembering midnight feasts, crushes on boys, sneaking banned music into our dorm rooms, and friendships that have spanned the years. The memories are not all idyllic, but I wouldn't trade them for all the wealth of Saudi Arabia. Added to these are memories of the pure beauty of Murree, a hill station nestled in the foothills of the Himalayan mountains. Our school building was an old Anglican church, restructured with classrooms off the auditorium. During the monsoon season, the rain pounded so hard on the tin roof that we would occasionally have to suspend class to save the voice of the teacher. During summers our boarding school community swelled to include parents from all over Pakistan, the United Arab Emirates, and Bangladesh. The boarding school version of community was strong and left an indelible mark on my life.

Despite growing up in a country that legally was not mine, a country that demanded visas and paperwork for long-term stays, I faced little loneliness. I belonged. These were my communities. And as an adult I found myself embracing strong expatriate communities in both Islamabad and Cairo, communities that functioned in much the same way as the groups in my childhood.

As I sat at our local Starbucks with sunlight pouring through the window and slow jazz music playing in the background, I thought about community. Across the room, a poster in the window invited readers to "Make a Career out of Connecting" "Apply now for a position!" it continued. The position was as a barista at this particular Starbucks.

"Community" and "Connection" are an integral part of the vocabulary of this country. We are encouraged to be part of a school community, a work community, a church community, the community of our town, a community that gardens, or a community that cooks. Pick the organization or the interest, add the word community, and bam! You have your very own community. Community should be "organic," a living, breathing organism, we are told. But as a kid I don't remember people talking about community. They just did it.

Connection is similar. We have Facebook connections, Linked-In connections, Twitter connections and Tumblr connections.. We connect by voice, text, email, g-chat, and Skype. We connect for coffee, at happy hours, for dinner.

But with all of these communities and all of these connections, why are so many of us so lonely?

I ponder this often. I work with people with chronic illness. I facilitate sessions that help them manage their chronic conditions. And in the first session, without fail, the participants admit to an overwhelming sense of loneliness, alienation, and defeat. It doesn't matter if they have five hundred friends on Facebook or two hundred and fifty names in their cell phone contact list. Ultimately they feel alone and sad.

What's the solution? I'm not sure. But I do know that more connections don't yield companionship, and that more words that tag community on to the end of them don't create friendships. And I do know that we are created for connection, soul connection, to God to other people, for "God sets the lonely in families, he leads forth the prisoners with singing" (Psalm 68:6)

Home [sick] for the Holidays

You cannot predict it. It's invisible. The symptoms are not obvious like a cold, a fever, a stomach ache. It comes on swiftly and unexpectedly, overwhelms immediately. It seems uncontrollable, comes by surprise, and brings intense pain. Physical symptoms – inability to concentrate, dry mouth, feeling of being close to tears all the time, not sleeping well – come later. Initially it is invisible. Homesickness.

For me it arrived on Christmas Eve. Suddenly our normal expat life and activities in Cairo were not enough. We needed family. We needed aunts, uncles, grandmas, grandpas, cousins, the people who aren't allowed to not like you, the ones glued to us by family bonds whether we like it or not.

As our young family left the candlelight Christmas Eve service, I felt a catch in my throat. Suddenly we didn't seem like enough for each other. We were too small, too fragile, unable to make it on our own.

Christmas day was alive with activity. We would attend my friend Betsy's annual open house. We would talk, and eat, assemble their mandatory Christmas puzzle, and sip the only spiked eggnog in Egypt. Christmas day never felt lonely or alone. Christmas Eve was the challenge.

Even as I write this, I know there are those of you whose throats are catching and tears welling up, tears that you try to push back into your tear ducts. While everyone else is home, you are homesick. You can just taste your sister's mulled wine, hear your mom's voice, picture the scene in a living room. It's you who are making a home in other parts of the world, creating wonder in a foreign land. This essay is for you.

My friend Martha has lived overseas for many years and understands the joys and challenges that come with the expatriate life. She writes this and I offer it to you:

> It was Christmas 1981. I was pregnant with Jeremy and horribly ill with constant morning sickness and facing the holiday knowing that it would be three years before we would see our families again. We didn't have a car yet (we were using a staff member's motorcycle), had lived without electricity in our maisonette for weeks. There was a bitter-sweetness as Mark and I made aluminum foil decorations and tried to find humble gifts to buy each other in Nairobi. Then how happy we were when a staff family invited us over to spend Christmas Day with them with a turkey dinner and a day of great food, playing games and talking. I felt like I had been transported back to America and to family. I felt God's mercy that day and the hope of joy and his love.

May you who are homesick, fighting back tears, not sure what this season will hold, feel God's mercy, the hope of joy, and His all-sufficient, never-ending, constantly surprising love.

Packing Up

We've packed up our cottage in Rockport. For the next nine months it will be occupied by another family. It works well this way. For nine months we have help paying the mortgage. For three summer months, we use and enjoy it.

In the last five years, "The Cottage" has become an important place in our family, a place of rest, memories, and ice cream, a place of favorite foods, Dutch Blitz, and Take Two, a place where we sleep late, read, and walk to ocean rocks. Even though I know renting out this space is wise, it's hard. It hurts.

There have been times in my life where I have dismissed feelings like this, feelings of loss of place. I have pushed them aside with the spiritual rebuke "after all, this world isn't my 'real' home. I'm told there is one far better…." but those voices of self, and sometimes others, have fallen flat into a guilty sort of sorrow. It has been in recent years that I have been willing to grieve the loss of place in a healthier way.

From the beginning of time, humans have been connected to places. We are born into place. How many times in a lifetime do we answer to the question "Where were you born?" or fill out a questionnaire or application that asks the same? Indeed the stories of our lives are intimately connected to place – the place you first kissed your husband or wife, the place where you first lived as a married couple, the place of your first memory, the place of first spiritual experiences, the place where a death occurred, the place of your first house, place of citizenship – pivotal and personal events, all connected to place.

We are confined and defined by place.

Paul Tournier addresses this need for place in his beautiful book *A Place For You*. A Swiss psychiatrist and a Christian with a wisdom that goes far beyond his psychiatric training, he says that to be human is to need a place, to be rooted and attached to that place. We are "incarnate beings" and so when those places are taken away, we suffer from a "disruption" of place. If the disruption goes beyond our ability to adapt it becomes a pathology - Tournier calls this a "deprivation of place."

To me this is a profound description of the global nomad, the person who moves from place to place. Many of us consider all the places where we've lived a source of pride, of identity. And they are. – But losing those places has a deep impact on our lives. And if not worked through, the "deprivation" of place gives way to profound grief and struggles with identity.

One of the beauties of Tournier's book is that in all the discussion of place there is woven a poignant reminder that God chooses "place" to reveal himself to people, to show who He is, to remind them of his love, his care, his sovereignty, to call them to himself.

Tournier gives no easy answers; the last chapter of the book is titled "The Problem is still difficult." Instead of trying to give an inadequate answer, he brings the reader continually back to God and place, reminding us that in God we are given full understanding and allowance of a need for place. And within that allowance, he asks us to trust Him.

So as I pack up place, I am grateful for the wisdom of this book; grateful for a God who somehow knows that we need place - place to grow, place to love, place to laugh, and place to worship. For even as I experience loss and the inconsistency of place I learn paradoxically of the constancy of God.

Between Worlds

Just being brought up by people who didn't and still don't feel fully here, fully present—that's very intense.

It's not just all about the house we live in and the friends we have right here. There was always a whole other alternative universe to our lives. Jhumpa Lahiri
The Quiet Laureate — Time Magazine 2008

If I could pick two words to describe my life, they would be the words "Between Worlds." Like a tightrope walker suspended between buildings, so was my life. My tightrope was between Pakistan and the United States; between home and boarding school; between Muslim and Christian.

Since birth I lived in a culture in between. Airports and airplanes were perfect places of belonging, because in the transit lounge with my books and my brothers, or at thirty thousand feet buckling and unbuckling my seatbelt in row 33D I was literally between worlds.

I always knew I would raise my children overseas. It was a given. It made complete sense. This was a world I loved, and surely my kids would love it too.

But there is a curious dynamic when an adult third culture kid raises third culture kids. I transferred my love of travel, adventure, languages, and cross-cultural living. I didn't worry that they would be away from their passport countries. I didn't worry that they would miss aunts and uncles. I knew theirs would be a life that few understand, and even fewer would experience. And I knew that the benefits would outweigh the deficits.

I was set. My world was a world of expatriate comings and goings, making friends with Egyptians, conjugating verbs in Arabic classes, and attending events at international schools. It was a world of change and transience and we were at home within that transience. We didn't name the losses. We didn't think there were any.

Then we moved. We left our home in Cairo of seven years, our life overseas of ten years, and moved to a small town in New England. A town that boasted of community and of Victorian homes, of a small school and of tidy lawns. A town with white picket fences and white faces.

And with this move the dynamic changed. I could no longer transfer what I knew to my children. Instead I transferred insecurity and an overpowering sense of other-ness

Nothing in my background had prepared me for this move. No books, no language classes, no articles. Nothing. I was struggling to find my way in a world that I didn't know, and I was doing it with five third culture kids on my apron strings. And suddenly this adult third culture kid thing was not an asset. It was a deficit, a glaring deficit that manifested itself in insecurity and turmoil. I didn't know how to cook with American ingredients or what to do at American public schools. Birthday parties and play dates were unfamiliar. My background was a conversation stopper.

What happens when the adult third culture kid finds herself raising third culture kids in their legal passport country? A whole lot of pain happens, a whole lot of insecurity, a whole lot of self-questioning and self-doubt. I hid all of this in a well-developed fortress of confidence, dressed up in up-to-date outfits that belied the out-of-date person I was. I worked hard to create a persona that would work. And I was exhausted. I wanted to curl up with my own mom and cry until the tears could fall no more. I wanted to gather my children to myself and whisk them off where we would be safe. I wanted to flee to Pakistan or Egypt, to my safe spaces.

But I did none of those things. I kept putting one foot in front of the other, step by blistered step. I made curry and Egyptian *Kosherie*, tastes of home in a strange land. I decorated with brass, copper, pottery, and a little double heart frame that stood on the mantel with pictures of Arafat and Rabin. We talked Egypt and Pakistan and slowly learned to talk small town New England. Our kids continued to say they were from Egypt, they were African American, they were 'different.' Our home was, in the words of Jhumpa Lahiri, an 'alternative universe' that stood in stark contrast to the world where we had unpacked our suitcases.

While America was on the outside, we had a whole other world on the inside. We continued to live in the space between, the one where I was most comfortable, between worlds. We looked like everyone around us, but we were immigrants in our own right. Negotiating two worlds was more than slightly schizophrenic and at times impossible.

I was a third culture kid raising third culture kids, and I wasn't sure how else to do it. But Grace entered the space between, and slowly by slowly I began to meet people who wanted to hear my story, who shared our curry, who walked beside me. Slowly I began to trust these friends to be cultural brokers, liaisons who could explain American oddities to me so that I could feel more comfortable. And as I grew more comfortable, others grew more comfortable around me, around us. We no longer exuded a "We're other, we're better" scent. Instead, we could laugh and be content in our otherness, be accepted as different but not bad.

Years later I read, an article by Nina Sichel, words that reminded me of our story, that described what a third culture kid, raising third culture kids, needs:

> So when she comes to you, don't ask her where she's from, or what's troubling her. Ask her where she's lived. Ask her what she's left behind. Open doors. And just listen. Give her the time, space, and permission she needs to remember and to mourn. She has a story — many stories. And she needs and deserves to be heard, and to be healed, and to be whole.

That's what I needed, that's what they gave, and that's how I healed.

Lost to a Call

"We were Called." The words are heavy with spiritual meaning. They speak of deep times of prayer, of searching scripture, of agonizing over decisions, and of seeking guidance.

And those words can be lethal to a child. The child of missionaries operates between worlds – between the worlds of passport country and country of calling, between the worlds of school and home, between the worlds of Christian and Non-Christian, between the worlds of God's call and family needs. Always between worlds.

We were molded and shaped by parents who loved us and were called to a work that included a bigger, broader world, a world where "nine to five" or "weekend" were unknown.

And in some families, the broader, bigger world won. And the children lost. They were sacrificed to a greater commission, a higher calling of well-meaning parents whose hearts flamed with a passion. And the inevitable identity struggle that comes later in life became even more difficult, for the parent's strong, but perhaps misguided, sense of calling continues to figure significantly in the third culture kid's sense of self.

As I reflect on this I think about my own parents. They too had a call, they too answered a challenge posed to them in college. "Will you go?" "Will you leave family, security, belonging, home and go to a country that you don't know for the sake of the Gospel message?" They too lived between the broader world of being a part of a mission community and the smaller world of us, the Brown Family.

Why was I not lost to a Call? I'm not sure. But I know this. The call never superseded our needs. I was never told that I was in boarding school for the sake of the Gospel. In the deep places of my heart I knew that if I needed my parents, they would be there. Pakistan was precious. Their children more so. Somehow, for us, love won.

Calling had an upper, not a lower-case, "C." Mom and dad's Calling was to God Himself, and that would never change. That call was irrevocable. The call to Pakistan was lower-case. If they had to leave, God was still God. Their ability to stay in Pakistan might change, but the Call of God would never change. And God's Call included their children.

I have spoken and cried with missionary kids who were lost to a call, kids who love their parents but struggle to reconcile their sense of loss and abandonment with their faith, a faith shaped by a lower-case call. Even as I write this, I struggle. For as a parent I know what a struggle it is to live out a faith that is winsome, not destructive, to live out a passion for God that brings the family alongside, not sprawled in the dust.

But God is Big, bigger than our experiences, larger than our losses. He loves us more than any earthly parent ever could. And those who feel they were lost to a call often end up found by the God who Calls.

Is Calling in our DNA?

"So," said the kindly woman at the Baptist church, "you must want to be a missionary too when you grow up!" I hoped she couldn't see the visible distress on my face. She was so kind. How could I disappoint? But no, I didn't. I didn't want to be a missionary when I grew up. I didn't want to raise support. I didn't want to go from church to church in small New England towns. I did not want prayer letters or 'deputation.' No. I was eighteen. I wanted college and boyfriends and travel and stamps in my passport. And then down the road? Down the road I wanted to go overseas again. I just wasn't sure in what capacity.

Missionary kids and their parents bear two heavy burdens. The first is behavior. Missionary kids have just as many reasons to rebel as any other kid. More, some might argue. Our world contains pitfalls that can catch and take us down. I know. I was one who found marijuana growing in the back of Holy Trinity church, that noble and historic church in the town of Murree that the entire missionary community attended every summer. It is easy for us to hide behind the uniqueness of our experience. And then it's easy for a parent to feel guilt. "If we hadn't brought our kids half way around the world, this surely wouldn't have happened…" But in reality, when a kid is bent on bending rules it's going to happen anywhere.

The second burden is 'calling.' Calling is a word loaded with question marks and misunderstanding. My parents were called. Called first to God Himself, second to a life of service that took them places where all was initially unfamiliar. Foods, clothing, housing, plumbing, language, faith expression — all of it was new. It had to be learned and learned with humility and willingness to admit mistakes.

Along the way they had babies. And sometimes more babies. And what had been unfamiliar to them was home to their children. We first heard words and phrases in English, Urdu, and Sindhi. Curry was a staple, the call to prayer our first alarm clock. None of this spelled strange, it was all familiar.

But pressure that this would be our 'calling' simply because we were the children of missionaries was uncomfortable. On the one hand it seemed to make sense, like a family business where one by one the kids take their place behind the counter. But how many kids actually end up in the family business? How many children of nurses, teachers, and mechanics become nurses, teachers, or mechanics? Some do. But others follow another path, walk a different journey.

Ultimately the call of God isn't a business, it isn't an occupation. It's a unique word, heard in the heart and obeyed with the mind and body. A unique word that is planted and watered until it grows into an active, living, breathing call.

Missionary kids are called. But they are called to God Himself. After that, it's anyone's guess. After that it could be to a small town in England, a large city in North America, a tenured professorship at a university, a foreign service position with the state department. Rarely does our call look the same as that of our parents. Our journey often begins through the faith and calling of our parents, rooted in the past but grown and sustained through our own decisions of faith.

Is calling in our DNA? Threaded through each strand of our DNA is indeed a Call, a Call to "Glorify God and enjoy Him forever." Only this Call is carefully entwined in our spiritual genetic code from head to toe, from heart to soul.

And after that it's anyone's guess.

Mended Teapots

There are many treasures available in bazaars in Pakistan. Sometimes the smallest village would end up having the most amazing finds. A small oil lantern made of an old Coca-Cola can; antique brass with years of dust and tarnish; old scales perfect for a child's toy or a living room piece. Sometimes the treasure was simply discovering what Pakistanis saw as normal recycling.

Sometime in the eighties an expatriate realized while drinking chai at a local chai shop that the teapot on his table had been broken into many pieces but repaired painstakingly and put back together with metal staples along with a metal base making it reusable. He was amazed. It was a new and fascinating picture of recycling.

Taking the broken, mending it, reinforcing, and ending up with a product far stronger than the original.

He wanted one and it would be so easy to get. All he had to do was go home and break one of the small teapots his wife used for morning tea.

This he did and took the pieces to the local bazaar, asking around for a shopkeeper that would know this art. He quickly found one and was told to come back in two days for the repaired item. On return, to his dismay he found that the shopkeeper had assumed he wanted the repair done as well as possible and so left off the staples and the base. He requested that the shopkeeper add those — it was, after all, what had caught his attention in the first place, and he returned home with his prized possession.

As often happens in expatriate communities, once he found this treasure the rest of the community began looking for and finding these teapots in local bazaars. They were a charming addition to rooms already full of interesting objects, all with a story to go with them. We purchased one and, delighted with the find, set it on a bookshelf much to the surprise of Pakistanis who visited our home.

I love this teapot. You can see the cracks everywhere, large staples are placed over the cracks, and the metal base ensures a strong foundation.

Though broken and having little of its original beauty it is so much more interesting and represents so well the human condition. Despite the original break, despite the cracks it continues to be useable and stronger than if it had never been broken.

Very little could hurt this little pot. It is now twenty three years old and has traveled around the world from Pakistan to Florida, Florida to Egypt, Egypt to Massachusetts, Massachusetts to Phoenix, and Phoenix back to Massachusetts.

My life parallels that of the teapot. Through moves and crises, along with hundreds of cups of tea, it has survived. The teapot now sits on our shelf in Cambridge, ever a reminder that life can crack and mar us but it doesn't have to destroy.

Singing Songs in a Foreign Land

By the rivers of Babylon we sat and wept
    when we remembered Zion.
        There on the poplars
        we hung our harps,
    for there our captors asked us for songs,
    our tormentors demanded songs of joy;
they said, "Sing us one of the songs of Zion!"
    How can we sing the songs of the Lord
        while in a foreign land?
        If I forget you, Jerusalem,
    may my right hand forget its skill.
May my tongue cling to the roof of my mouth
        if I do not remember you,
        if I do not consider Jerusalem
            my highest joy.

In Psalm 137 the Psalmist gives us a picture of a people displaced, in exile. They are by a river and they are weeping. They hang up their musical instruments and those around them shout at them to sing songs, songs of joy. "Pull up your bootstraps people! Sing songs of joy. It's not that bad!"

151

But the Psalmist disagrees. He says this: "How can we sing the songs of the Lord while in a foreign land?"

Many third culture kids and expats have uttered the same words. How can I sing? How can I praise? I'm displaced. I don't like where I live. I hurt inside and no one on the outside knows. I don't fit. I feel like an alien among humans. How can I sing?

Perhaps our unspoken fear is that if we learn to sing songs of joy in this new place, this new land, then we will forget the old, we will lose our identity, all that we know, all that is familiar. As one person put it: "I wanted to preserve my identity, to hold dear the soil in which my roots are settled, to Never Forget who I Am. After all — my identity has come at such a high cost."

Yet this is the beauty of a God of movement, a God of place. He is not limited by geography. He created time and space, he created place. He is the author of our identity. Our physical location may change, but our song can still go on. The song may change, it may become more of a song of remembrance, but it can still be a song of joy.

God does not ask us to forget. He knows that from birth we were raised between worlds, that those worlds shaped who we are — not only physically and emotionally, but also spiritually. He simply asks us to move forward and trust him. Trust him with our shifting loyalties to place, trust that he will allow us to use the gifts that were so naturally used in the past, trust that the hidden talents of language and cultural adaptation will not be wasted. Trust that it is possible to love more than one place at a time, that it is possible to sing songs of joy in both.

That is my prayer for you who read this book — that wherever we may be we will learn to sing songs of joy in a foreign land.

Culture Clash

Cultural values and views constantly intersect when living between worlds. Driving into an intersection takes awareness of traffic laws and attention to all those on the road to avoid a collision. Cultures intersecting need the same degree of attention. At every intersection there is potential for collision, in every cross-cultural encounter there is potential for the same.

Cereal Aisle Paralysis

If there is a common thread of experience among third culture kids it may be paralysis in the cereal aisle.

I walk into the local chain supermarket and grab a shopping cart. The vegetable and fruit section cause minimal trauma, despite my instinct to bargain with the produce manager. But trouble begins when I turn the corner into aisle three. A sea of cereal assaults me. The sizes, colors, names, and food labels blend into a kaleidoscope. I want to cry. I am paralyzed. I can't choose. In that instant I am transported back to Esajee and Sons, the small general store on Mall Road in Murree.

In the summers, I accompanied my mother to Esajee's. It was all so simple. My mother would give Mr. Eesajee a list, and he would climb a ladder, pulling down items one by one: Lyle's Golden Syrup, Nice biscuits, Digestive biscuits, Green's cheddar cheese, butter, and Fauji Corn flakes. Fauji Corn Flakes was one of two choices of cold cereal available in the market. They immediately became soggy when touched by a drop of milk, and the nutritional value was perhaps minimal, but it was all we had, and we were content. And if given a choice, I would always pick *parathas* and omelets at a local teashop.

I'm jarred back to my present reality by an announcement over the loudspeaker. I have no idea how long I have been standing still, or how many people have passed me by. If I survive this paralysis and make up my mind, there are some good tasting cereals in aisle three, all available for a price. I begin to read names and labels. I pick Cheerios and Honey Bunches of Oats. Then I am looking through the kaleidoscope again. There are fifteen kinds of granola on the shelf.

Why the cereal aisle? The bread aisle has many choices. So does the jam and jelly section. What is it about cereal that brings out the confusion and paralysis, the feeling of being alone? It should all be so simple. Third culture kids are among the brightest people I have met. We survive wars, rumors of wars, and military coups; we know how to bargain in three or more languages; we can sleep anywhere and eat things that would send many to the hospital. Why can't we pick cereal? Why is the mundane so hard?

In ordinary life we develop skills that are not easily transferable across cultures. Sleeping on a roof-top under mosquito netting on hot nights. Making mayonnaise with a blender. Long periods of separation from family. Eating fish curry with our hands. Fifteen hour flights. Vacationing in Axis-of-Evil countries. Coping with apparently insurmountable crises. These are normal. These are our ordinary life.

No wonder our lives feel challenged by the normal in our passport countries. No surprise that it is difficult to make peace with the commonplace. In my case, recovery begins with the miracle of movement. People who have experienced severe accidents with trauma to the spinal cord will often say that learning to walk again is one of the hardest things they have ever done. Physically I cannot pretend to relate, but emotionally I know exactly what this is like. We must learn to walk all over again, learn to live differently, first in baby steps, gradually gaining strength and momentum. It takes time and it takes work.

The cereal aisle is my baby step in the journey. Once I have picked my cereal, refusing to give in to the feelings of immobility, I find the rest of my grocery shopping goes quite smoothly. I decide to pass on the granola. Enough trauma for one day.

Stories Matter

There is no other people in the world (says one Eastern traveller) who love a good story so well, and are so excited by hearing romantic tales, as the Arabs. Source unknown

When our children were younger and we lived in the Middle East we bought a series of children's books that told tales from the Arabian Nights. Boasting titles like *Ali Baba and the Forty Thieves, The Story of Aladdin and the Wonderful Lamp,* and *Sinbad the Sailor,* they were adapted from the larger book *One Thousand and One Nights* — otherwise known as *Arabian Nights.*

Although adapted, these books were not dumbed-down. They were long, intricate and involved. They told complex tales of thievery and deception, longing and love. If we wanted to put our children to bed quickly we did not opt for these tales as their bedtime story.

One day as I was reading one of these books to my children I started thinking about how much more enjoyable they were than some of the Western children's books that we had on our shelf. Most of them couldn't compete with the stories from "*One Thousand and One Nights.*"

The longer we lived in the Middle East, the more our family loved these stories. And we began to spin our own tales. All true at the core but, like any good story-teller, we embellished them with rich additions that made the telling and the remembering all the better. Whether at Cairo coffee houses or around expatriate dinner tables, good stories were plenty and memorable.

I am more and more certain that part of adjusting to a new country, a new world, is being able to tell stories of the old world. The more we are able to share our stories, the more quickly we come to see our new surroundings as homes. We become stronger and more secure through telling our stories.

When we moved to the United States after three years in Pakistan and seven years in Egypt, we came with a lot of stories. We had birthed and raised five kids on three continents. We had swum in the Red Sea and picnicked by the Pyramids; we had traveled to Istanbul, and lunched in the Plaka in Athens; we had drunk cocktails with ambassadors and shared bread with refugees. All of those stories were consolidated into our twenty six suitcases as we moved to a house with the address Two Main Street.

But behind the Victorian house on Main Street was a family whose stories didn't go away, they were still there, but the listeners were few. It felt like too much to ask of a provincial place where we were the outsiders.

Into that world came friends who understood our need and listened to our stories. They ate curry with us and challenged my view that no one raised in the West could make a good curry by showing up with one of the best Thai curries I have yet to eat. They loved us and brought us gently into their world. And as we were brought into their world, we began to relax and to realize that we were accepted with all our stories and all our idiosyncratic quirks picked up from years of living in different cultural contexts.

They were cultural brokers bridging gaps of understanding and making us feel welcome. I began to learn that you don't have to experience everything to be able to empathize and listen. And as I grew in comfort I no longer had to announce to the world before they had asked *"I'm not from here you know!"*

The more I hear from immigrants, refugees and third culture kids, the more I am convinced that communicating our stories is a critical part of adjusting to life in our passport countries. We have a lifetime of experiences that when boxed up for fear of misunderstanding, will result in depression and deep pain. As we tell our stories we realize that these transitions and moves are all a part of a bigger narrative, a narrative that is strong and solid and gives meaning to our lives. As we learn to tell our stories we understand not only the complexity of our experience, but the complexity of the human experience, the human heart. So we learn to tell our stories - because your story, my story, and our stories matter.

They Want our Symptoms, but not our Stories

"They want to know our symptoms, but they don't want to hear our stories," said the young Somali woman. It was a profound accusation, and as I took it in I realized that in many areas of life in the United States we have lost our respect for narrative. Wanting empirical data that can be weighed, measured, and argued, we grow impatient with words and long descriptions. We had been talking about healthcare, about communicating with nurses and doctors. But the accusation is not just about healthcare.

For many, symptoms are best understood within the context of a story. Many people from other parts of the world don't see symptoms as a list to recite. Rather, they see the symptoms as part of the whole, and the whole includes eating *paella* at a grandmother's house five days ago.

I got it! I understood exactly what my patient was saying. I have my own experience of the importance of the story when treating the patient. On arrival in the United States, I quickly realized that our children would not be able to attend school unless they were up to date on their immunizations. With this in mind, I made an appointment at the office of a pediatrician nearby. We drove in a bright red mini-van to the office with little yellow vaccination booklets in hand, documentation of their vaccines thus far.

Into the office I walked, with five kids aged one to eleven. Our kids had never seen anything like this doctor's office. Dr. Seuss books were arranged neatly on a bookshelf, toys were attractively put into square baskets lined with bright fabric. And to their wonder, beautiful, healthy, multi-colored fish filled an aquarium. Their last visit to a pediatrician's office had been a year before. We had taken the long taxi ride to Cairo's Mohandiseen neighborhood, and crowded in to a drab office filled with sick children. When it was our turn in the doctor's office, I explained that we had come to be weighed, measured and vaccinated. The doctor was incredulous. "Do you see how busy I am? And how sick are the children waiting to see me? We don't have vaccines for healthy children like yours!" Shame-faced I made some sort of tepid reply that I wanted to make sure they were growing as per a growth chart. The session ended well with both of us laughing and I was on my way, kids in tow, happy that they had not had to have a needle poke them.

This is what I thought of as we waited to see the doctor in this small town in New England. Then our names were called and the six of us traipsed in, proud in newly purchased outfits and shoes, ready to take on our role in the United States. The busy and zealous nurse didn't make eye contact, but raised her eyebrows in unspoken accusation. I should have used better birth control.

I began telling our story. Our story of Pakistan, then Cairo, and now the United States. I told it so she would understand the empty spaces on a vaccine record that in America would have been filled. She nodded her head. "I'm not listening honey," her nod communicated, "but you just go on talking!"

And then suddenly she stopped examining the records. She now made eye contact and there was no mistaking the accusations. "Your children are under immunized," she announced. "Yes," I stammered. "As I said, we've been living overseas and they didn't have vaccines when I went to the doctors..." I trailed off. Her eyes went back and forth between children and yellow vaccine records, children and yellow vaccine records. Then they meaningfully shifted to me. "In this country we call that neglect" she said. Her voice was clear, her meaning more so.

My world and children flashed before my eyes. I didn't know a lot about living in the United States, but I did know the word neglect and the meaning behind it. In the United States neglect carries a weight of accusation and fear, the spectre of a hostile visit from social services. It's terrifying.

Neglect? Neglect? The words echoed through the small room. I was saved from having to respond by her zealous body rising and leaving the room telling me over her shoulder that she would discuss this with another nurse and be back. Tears filled my eyes. Tears that I had to squash because there were children who I loved to the core of my being with me, and they knew something was not right.

The minutes that passed seemed like a lifetime as I pictured my children removed from my home and placed in a home where vaccine records were stamped in little yellow books by a stone-faced person.

My thought picture was interrupted by a new nurse. Within seconds, I realized that my worry would not materialize. She began asking questions, and I began telling our story. The conversation switched from where we were to where we had been. She didn't just care about our present, she cared about our past, and our past had everything to do with our current reality. Within a short time, we had an immunization schedule and we were on our way.

Stories and symptoms are intertwined. If we don't hear the story, we don't see the patient in context. A friend of mine has done a great deal of research on the importance of understanding a patient's cultural background in order to treat them effectively. He believes three factors – curiosity, empathy, and respect – are critical to providing culturally responsive care to patients. If any one of these is missing, we miss the full picture.

Our second nurse showed curiosity, empathy, and respect. She learned where we had been so she could meet us where we were now. In her zeal, the first nurse missed the heart of the story.

Being able to tell this story has been part of a healing process in my heart, more evidence of the power of narrative, the power of stories. And every time I tell this story, I am more determined to be the second nurse, the nurse that cared about the story, the nurse that displayed curiosity, empathy and respect.

The Language of Care

Within two weeks of our arrival in Cairo my son Joel fell and hit his forehead on the sharp corner of a bed. The resulting inch long gash was on his eyebrow. His beautiful blue toddler eyes were unharmed.

I pride myself that I tend to "stay calm and carry on." I am, after all, a nurse. But I was new to Cairo, new to Arabic and I forgot for a moment that I was a nurse. What I remembered was that I had no car, no money, no friends and my husband was off to work, forty-five minutes away, at the university job he had begun a week before.

I called the one person I knew, a man we met on arrival in Cairo and frantically asked him which hospital he would recommend from his senior position of having lived in the country two years longer than we had. He told me to head to El Salaam, a hospital ten minutes away by taxi on the corniche of the Nile River. In a moment of compassion, he offered to drive us, and I gratefully accepted.

Wanting to find someone to watch my other children, I ran to check with the only other English-speaking family in the six-story building. They were not home. A mother and daughter from France were living on one of the lower floors. I rushed down to see if this would work. My French is practically non-existent. Monsieur Morgan's French class in ninth and tenth grade while on a home leave in the United States had equipped me to say *"C'est la vie!"* emphatically, and *"Ou est la grande fromage?"* equally emphatically. Under the circumstances that didn't do much. But in the language of a mom's frantic heart I was able to communicate enough so that they came running upstairs to help and told me (I think) to be on my way. I will never really know what they said.

Minutes later, I was trying, desperately, to explain what had happened to the hospital staff. I used many hand motions, Joel used many tears, and the blood told the rest of the story. When the doctor arrived, I was incredibly grateful for his fluent English and wonderful bedside manner. We were safe.

I think about this story when I'm working in health care settings with immigrants or refugees who have limited English. In emergencies, we forget second languages; our default is to go to our first language, the language that is most familiar. We forget everything but that need for help.

And while the default for the patient limited in language skills is to revert to her first language, the default for the health professional is to get louder. We seem to think, illogically, that if we talk louder, the person's English will somehow get better. As ridiculous as we know this is, we nevertheless do it.

Joel bears the scar of that day. It is a badge of childhood. It could have been far worse. We were treated with kindness and efficiency. The doctor, skilled with the needle closed up the wound with little stitches. I still see my son's bright blue eyes looking at me throughout the process. He was so brave.

When I returned to the United States I found myself in opposite circumstances. I was now the one who spoke the language and patients coming to the health center were just as I was in Cairo, new to the country, new to the language, with no cars, no friends and no money. It's a role reversal. And during those interactions I remember that emergency room visit.

This memory of kindness in the face of difference serves as an example to me, for I too was a newcomer, a stranger, and experienced grace spoken through the language of care

Holy Moments from an Unholy Disaster

Given the choice of a five star hotel or camping, I will pick a five star hotel. I tell friends that anyone who grew up in the developing world with a commode for a toilet and one bath a week would appreciate my love of luxury. So it was with some surprise that I found myself eager to return to Pakistan on a medical flood relief team.

When I first heard news of the floods, I felt a sadness that was somewhat distant and removed. Pakistan was my childhood love and home, but as an adult I have been more connected to the Middle East through work and travel. My connections with Pakistan had been reduced to occasional emails from friends and to moments on the subway when, eyes closed, the rhythmic movement transports me back to the Pakistani trains of my childhood. That changed when I saw a picture in the *New York Times* of the city of Jacobabad under floodwaters.

Jacobabad, in the Sindh province, was home to my family when I was a little girl. I broke my leg there. My mother's artificial flowers were stolen in Jacobabad. Mom had planted them around our house to add color to clay that would never grow anything. They provided a source of joy for a few hours and then they were gone. The *New York Times* photograph hit my heart in a way I had not anticipated, and through what could only be a work of God an opportunity came about for me to participate as a nurse on a medical relief trip to care for internally displaced people in northern Sindh. I never imagined that my life for a short time would resemble a *National Geographic* feature story.

Although I grew up in Pakistan, raised my family in Islamabad, and lived for seven years in Cairo, my current reality is downtown Boston, where I drink a Starbucks coffee daily. I shop at Ann Taylor and get frustrated when my hot water runs out or I don't have time to put on my eyeliner. But in early September the idea of working with victims of the flood suddenly became real and I became cautiously excited, knowing I may not have what it would take but willing to take that chance.

On October fifteenth, accompanied by my sister-in-law, Carol, and thirteen thousand dollars worth of donated medical supplies, I boarded an Etihad airliner and flew via Abu Dhabi to Karachi ending the journey in Shikarpur, Sindh. Outside the Shikarpur gates, a kilometer from the hospital where we were based we passed the burnt remains of a convoy of twenty seven trucks that had been featured in the *New York Times* "Pictures of the Day," and I realized then that I hadn't paid as close attention to the location of that picture as I perhaps should have.

The two weeks that followed were filled with holy moments. I watched as a mom pointed to heaven in thanks for food distributed to her family. I laughed with children at my own mistakes in Urdu and Sindhi. I prayed in the depths of my soul for the baby who looked like a skeleton at four months of age and for the emaciated mom who held that child with the love only a mother could have. I put shoes on the ulcerated feet of an ancient woman, countless stories written into the wrinkles on her face. We delivered a sewing machine to a widow who danced with it on her head. We saw so clearly that people are created in the image of God. These women and children in their unwashed yet beautiful bright colored clothing were "no mere mortals" and dear to the heart of God. Our team – a doctor, two nurses, a community healthworker, interpreter and food distributors – were like a mini United Nations. We represented six people groups and six different languages, but we shared a unity in purpose and spirit that gave us efficiency, laughter and joy. In fourteen days we covered eight villages, surveying needs, running medical camps, and distributing food. Mud huts, tents provided by USAID, and *charpais* combined with chickens, roosters, water buffalo and cow dung completed the setting and tested our nostrils and stamina. But everyday provided a new adventure and new moments of awe

There was, for me, an added bonus. Almost anyone who was raised in a country other than his or her passport country can relate with the immigrant experience. The sense of isolation, nontransferable skills and being 'other' can creep up at the oddest of times and result in a deep loneliness and sometimes conflict with one's passport country. Our lives are lived between worlds. But for those two weeks I was not other. I was home. I saw friends who knew me when I was young, received blessings from men who worked with my father and women who had deep friendships with my mother, walked through compounds to the embraces of old friends, and was woken yet again by the call to prayer. These were holy moments that I had not anticipated. A wise friend once told me that there are times in our lives when we need to remember who we are. During those two weeks, I was given the gift of remembering who I was.

Since leaving Pakistan as a child, I, like many, had to redefine my faith. It has often been a painful process. I struggle with unanswerable questions about life and God. This trip back was a humbling reminder that the God who sustained me when I was six years old at boarding school, crying into my pillow, is a God who still provides holy moments in places where real life happens.

I arrived back in JFK International Airport in New York City after twenty three hours of travel and within a few minutes felt 'other' again. I faced a moment of confusion as I looked at the Immigration line options. Was I really a resident alien? An alien? No. I was a US citizen, shaped by cultures and moments that were not of my own making. In that moment I recognized that the peace of belonging happens deep in my soul and that peace can transcend the outside circumstances.

I don't know why I was given the gift of going. That is a mystery to me. But I know it was Grace.

Capable of Complexity

Shivering, wrapped in a cotton shawl despite the heat of the day, the man sat uncomfortably on a stool in the makeshift clinic. Our clinic was in a mud house and consisted of a fold up table, three stools for doctor, patient, and interpreter, and a small bag with stethoscope, otoscope, and antibacterial hand cleanser.

He was miserable, shaking with fever and itching his skin. "May I examine your chest," asked Dr. Wendell. Rosina, the interpreter, looked at the doctor and shook her head. Rosina knew the answer even before she was asked. Dr. Wendell was a woman. "But I need to see his chest!" Dr. Wendell insisted. "In Pakistan culture . . ." began Rosina.

We had heard those words many times as we fumbled our way through medical needs, one hundred degree heat, and vast cultural differences. Cultural values were constantly intersecting and clashing during our IDP (Internally Displaced Person) medical relief camps. To avoid a collision, driving into an intersection requires awareness of traffic laws and attention to all those on the road. Cultural intersections require the same degree of attention. Every intersection brings potential for collision.

174

Rosina was not only an excellent interpreter but also a cultural broker, explaining and advising on areas that had potential for misunderstanding and misinterpretation. She would begin every informal lesson with "In Pakistan culture…" and then go on to tell us what was the norm. From family dynamics to seeing a doctor, the path had potential pitfalls. Patients were gracious to us as we fumbled our way though encounters, laughing at our language mix-ups and applauding when we used words or grammar correctly.

A man in this area of Pakistan, Rosina went on to explain, would not bear his chest to a woman, even a doctor. Resigned, Dr. Wendell did what she could within the confines of the culture.

The shock came as we left the village. Dr. Wendell, looking out the van window, cried out in astonishment, "But isn't that the same man?" There at the pump, his chest bared, wearing only a small, plaid *dhoti*, was our patient. Soaping up, taking a pump bath for the entire world to see, he was oblivious that the female doctor could finally see his chest.

Intersecting with cultures means being capable of complexity. Many in the United States are aghast at a woman breast-feeding in public. Yet no one looks twice at another scantily clad woman in a revealing tank top, half her breast bared. To a Western observer a man unwilling to let a female physician see his chest, yet bathing in public oblivious to the whole world doesn't seem to make sense. As humans, we have an unbelievable capacity for apparent hypocrisy and paradox. Olive oil is food in one culture, a hair care product in the next. In one culture an image is art, in another pornography. In one context taking a life is heroism, in another murder. We blast the Muslim World for veiling, calling it degrading, yet we eat up the news of actors and their playmates, congressman and their sexting. In the same breath, we praise one system of beliefs as tolerant, while blasting another for its narrowness. We are a people of contrasts and complexity.

In *Mountains Beyond Mountains* Paul Farmer tells the story of a research project on tuberculosis treatment in Haiti. Some patients took medication because they believed it could make them better, others were unconvinced and would only take it knowing there was a monetary incentive at the end of the treatment. In a conversation with one woman who had taken the medicine and was experiencing health and wellness, Dr. Farmer talked and laughed with her about those who thought that the disease was a result of a voodoo curse. "We know better than that" they agreed. Yet as Dr. Farmer was leaving, the woman remarked that she was still going to get back at the person who had cursed her and caused the disease. Dr. Farmer was astonished. Hadn't they just agreed that the disease had nothing to do with a curse, and everything to do with germs and the germ theory. She shook her head, smiled at him and said, "Cherie! Are you incapable of complexity?"

This section of the book has had a profound effect on me. The older I get the more I am aware that the complexity of our behavior is as old as life itself. As I navigate the worlds in which I live, I do well to remember and to ask myself, "My dear, are you incapable of complexity?"

The Lexicon of Normal

As my daughter Annie celebrated her twenty seventh birthday in Cairo, protesters stormed the US Embassy, climbed over the walls, and pulled down an American flag. They then tried to set the flag on fire outside the compound. This happened a few blocks away, a five to seven minute walk from Annie's apartment. In nearby Libya a far more serious attack occurred. J. Christopher Stevens, the United States Ambassador to Libya, and three other American diplomats died in that attack.

The events were deadly serious. But the conversation between Annie and her dad offered a humorous window into how third culture kids react to events that make it to the front page of newspapers worldwide. "Annie, are you ok? I just heard the embassy was stormed!" "Yeah, I'm fine. We're having my birthday party right now." In other words, life goes on.

Living through these headline events is sometimes easier than when a third culture kid hears about an event in a country they have lived and love, but they are thousands of air miles away.

A few years ago, when I learned of the terrorist attack on Murree Christian School, the school I attended from age five through age eighteen, I felt a little foolish at my reaction. It was as though I had left the school a year before instead of twenty five years ago. In *A Place for You* Paul Tournier writes that "A man becomes attached to his place, he becomes one with it. It becomes a part of his person, of his inner self, so that anything that happens to his place also affects his person." I was deeply affected by the attack because of the place Murree held in my life. At Murree I went from little girl to high school graduate. God chose Murree as the place where I would grow from child to adult, the place where I would learn more of him. In a symbolic way, that part of me felt attacked.. Murree would never be the same.

For the third culture kid, being present yet in possible danger is sometimes easier than being absent and safe. Being present means we are still a part of that fabric. We can still experience the event with like-minded people. Being absent means trying to convey to those around, who don't have the same emotional connection to that place, how deeply we are affected by the event.

Most of the third culture kids I know have lived through a minimum of one or two wars, political unrest, and at least one natural disaster. Stories are shaped around these events. Normal life goes. As embassies are stormed, birthday parties are held and the third culture kid has yet another event to add to her lexicon of normal.

Cab Driver Conversations

He was from Algeria. I never learned his name. His taxi had waited on the corner of the main road for who knows how long when I peered in the partly closed window and asked if he could take me home. I don't normally take taxis home. It's a silly expense. Home is just twelve minutes walking distance from where I was. But I was running late, and my hands were heavy with thin, green, recyclable, plastic bags from the market where I had shopped. As I struggled to get out of the car I asked him if he could come back in an hour to take me to the airport. He smiled and willingly agreed.

I scrambled to get ready, unpacking groceries, writing notes to the family, finding a lone earring here and a hairbrush there, doing the last-minute things that aren't that important but feel important at the time.

As promised, he returned. This is when I learned he was from Algeria. He moved to the United States fourteen years ago and lives in East Boston. He drives this cab daily, taking frantic women like me home from grocery shopping, transporting tourists to and from places, and making runs to the airport. Like most cab drivers, he works hard. He doesn't own his car but leases it, paying the fees out of his daily catch.

We began talking the way immigrants often talk. What was it like when you first came? Did you know English? Where did you live? How did you find work? The questions and answers flowed easily.

At one point, he had lived in a suburb south of Boston. We talked about the social isolation of the suburbs, how both of us were lonely when we lived with larger homes and gardens, but less community. "I see people," he said in an unmistakably Arabic accent, "and they make their money and they move. My friends say 'I can live in a house so much cheaper outside of the city.' And I look at them, and I say 'But you will be so lonely.' And they are!" Along with building malls and lovely houses surrounded by pristine lawns, we have also built walls of isolation, social and physical.

We talked about being strangers in the city, and the unlikely sense of belonging that comes with anonymity. We talked about being new in the country, not knowing the rules and having to pretend, pretend that we were happy, pretend that we knew what was going on, pretend that we had it together. And then we were at the airport, and I was grabbing my luggage and making sure I gave a big tip, a tip that showed appreciation not only for his work but also for the conversation. I smiled as I realized I had had a deeper conversation with this taxi driver than I have with people whom I know far better, whom I see every day.

I've not seen him again, but there have been other cab driver conversations, with Omar from Turkey, Ahmed from Egypt, Moustafa from Pakistan. They all come with a story, they all work hard, none of them own their cabs, all of them face grumpy passengers and long schedules. But they continue with a tenacity and resilience characteristic of immigrants.

Third culture kids, immigrants, refugees, foreigners. We find each other in unlikely spaces. In the shared experience of being other, we find belonging and rest, whether in a short ride to an airport or a long-distance phone conversation. These moments of connection seem to come at the right time, sustaining us until the next encounter, preventing us from falling into an abyss of self-pity and isolation.

Global Connections

On a sleepy, hot summer afternoon, I posted a note on a friend's Facebook wall. "Hey, did you know a girl at the International School in Islamabad who had her nose pierced? She was the one who first inspired me to get my nose pierced." This short, seemingly meaningless comment led to a remarkable series of global connections and memories from long ago. The Pakistan and Afghanistan of our youth was resurrected, and I was in happy awe. The same friend recently wrote in an essay: "Our reunion conversations are all over the boards. Politics and religion, poverty and wealth; we speak of riots and wars as other people speak of climbing trees and playing with dolls."

Third culture kids participate in a vast, global network of people, places, and events. Kevin Bacon's six degrees of separation reduces to three degrees or less. We create lists (You know you are a TCK when...) that bind us together in our global identities. We compare passports and war zone stories, we remember minute details that end up making sense to other third culture kids, yet seem silly to others. We put 'home' in quotes, and desperately seek out cultural brokers who can help us understand our passport countries. We talk about our friends who are ambassadors, peace negotiators or NPR reporters on Morning Edition. We find out that we knew the same people in Cairo, or Islamabad, or Delhi and attended the same interschool activities. We decorate with Persian carpets from Pakistan and Iran, brass from India, pottery from Turkey, and pictures from everywhere. We know goodbyes in a way we wish we didn't, and we struggle to articulate grief and loss. Yet in the next breath we speak of how we wouldn't give up the lives we've had for anything.

Yet despite all these global connections and airport journeys, despite having a passport full of stamps from nations around the world, we still struggle when ordering coffee in our passport countries.

Learning to Speak Coffee

"We are the cream of the crop in China and when we come here we don't even know how to order coffee!" a Chinese friend said to my husband. She's not alone in her struggle to figure out the seemingly 'normal.' Between our departure from the United States in 1986 and our return in 1996, a new language was adopted as an official second language. It seemed amazing that this could have occurred in a country full of "English Only" zealots, but it did. The language was "coffee" and it came with its own vocabulary, syntax, and idioms. What made it more confusing were the many dialects that existed, sometimes in the same neighborhood.

Coffee culture had grown beyond a simple drink with one or two minor variations and had developed a complex system of ritual and language, full of pitfalls. The result was that for two years I did not get the drink that I thought I had ordered. I was left with a feeling of stupidity. I would never master the task of learning to speak coffee. And because the language was most used in the context of tired people in long lines with morning breath, there was little patience for someone who was a learner.

While going through the language-learning process in

both Egypt and Pakistan, my feeble attempts grew more powerful each passing day as they were met with good humor and encouragement. Little smiles, gentle corrections, sometimes-outright laughter all helped guide me through verbs, adverbs, and adjectives, giving me confidence that Arabic and Urdu would indeed become easier. Not so in the land of Starbucks and Dunkin' Donuts. The vernacular was serious and there was nary a smile to go with it. But I had suffered bad coffee long enough. In a tearful moment, I swore that I would triumph. I would learn how to speak coffee, and my coffee would no longer be too sweet or not sweet enough, too strong or too weak. It would be perfect because I would learn this language that had eluded me, the language of coffee.

My strategy was simple. I would mimic. This had served me well in the past. I had a good ear and would listen. When it was my turn at the counter I would repeat verbatim what the person two spaces in front of me had ordered. One space in front felt too creepy. I didn't want others in line to suspect that I didn't know what I was doing.

The first day I nervously waited, listened carefully and then repeated exactly as I heard: "I'll take a grande triple shot soy vanilla latte."

Relieved I stepped away from the counter and waited. After what seemed far too long of a wait, my drink was ready and I took my first sip. I promptly spit it out. This was coffee? This had to be a joke. Defeated, I consoled myself that I was only on day one. There was a science to this. Eventually I was bound to get the perfect cup. My plan was to try for two weeks. Surely, at that point my language skills would have improved sufficiently to have decent coffee.

To my fascination two weeks into this experiment, I realized with a little thrill that I had three good cups of coffee in a row. Not only that, I had been to two different language groups so I knew both a primary dialect and a secondary dialect. More significantly, I was doing this without my voice catching, without the little tremble that made me feel like a five-year old who isn't completely catching on to hooked on phonics. My voice sounded strong and resilient, slightly arrogant and definitely knowing, the way the woman in front of me had sounded that morning with her perfectly coiffed hair and sophisticated black coat.

Who knew that a seemingly trivial thing like coffee would represent adjustment and effective living? The kind of angst it had evoked for such a long time was now over. What did it all mean? And though I didn't want to read too much into it, why did it feel so descriptive of my life? How shallow had I become?

As I've talked to others who are immigrants, or refugees or have returned from living abroad, they echo these fears about daily life. I realize that I'm not alone. Everyday tasks with unspoken rules are daunting and, on mastery, yield the greatest sense of triumph. For me it was coffee. Grocery shopping, public transportation, learning to drive years past the age of the teenagers who confidently take to the road, and banking may seem easy but they come with intense challenges and fears. It's easy to feel isolated and defeated. But that's no way to live life, nor is it the modus operandi of the third culture kid. We are described as resilient and flexible, able to adapt to new situations in a moment's notice. As we forge ahead wanting America or Canada or the UK or Germany to work for us, wanting to live effectively in our new surroundings, these every day skills are gradually learned. Sometimes they are mastered with excellence, and we slowly relax and make temporary peace with our surroundings.

My language skills are now incredible! I could pass a state department language exam with the two major coffee dialects that are present in my neighborhood. I speak with skill and confidence. But periodically when I'm tired and forget whether the adjective is grande or medium I'm reminded of the time when the language was new and I was struggling. It is at those times that I am inevitably in the queue with someone who has limited coffee speaking ability and an impatient crowd and I want to be bold enough to offer help. Sometimes that happens, but more often, I end up forgetting the language myself and find that I am once again drinking a bad cup of coffee.

Because Love is not Rude

The 60's and 70's were good decades to be an American growing up in Pakistan. We faced little animosity, and were often treated deferentially. As a child, I became adept at exploiting this deference. I'm not proud of this history.

One incident remains with me. It both characterizes me at that stage, and leaves me a model for parenting when a child behaves badly. I was around ten years old. We had just attended the Anglican Church in Hyderabad. Compared to village services this church was huge, with pews, high ceilings, and robed priests. After the service, Pakistani and European parishoners remained to chat, as was customary. The Anglican Church was in a walled compound and expatriate families from different parts of the world lived in some of the houses. Many were our friends.

All five of us kids were in the Land Rover that had carried us many miles through treacherous passes and along the equally treacherous Grand Trunk Highway. My parents were finishing a conversation, and we were doing what siblings do best: arguing, teasing, hair pulling. My brother Stan, who had an uncanny ability to both love, challenge, and annoy, was teasing me. I was responding when two teenage Pakistani siblings, a brother and a sister, walked by, saw us, and laughed. I didn't skip a beat, I promptly redirected my frustration at the teasing to them and stuck my tongue as far out as it could go, fingers in ears, eyes squinted for effect. I added an exaggerated, mocking expression to top it off. Immediately the car erupted. "I'm telling mom and dad!" four brothers hollered at once. One thing we knew, mom and dad would have no rude behavior directed at Pakistanis. None. That was crossing a line. I knew I was in big trouble.

At that moment mom and dad made their way back to the car. Four male eye-witnesses relayed the story, probably tripping over each other to get their bratty sister in trouble. My father was furious. The minute we got home, I got the hardest spanking of my childhood. I had crossed a line and my parents needed me to know that this was unacceptable behavior. In a country where we were guests and treated hospitably, with great kindness, my rude actions would not be tolerated – because Love is not rude and does not demand its own way.

I've never forgotten that spanking. My parents were correct in their punishment. A mere scolding would never have carried the impact needed to get their point across. It was far too easy for me, a white American child, to consciously or subconsciously develop a superior attitude purely because of the color of my skin and my country of origin. And that superiority was wrong.

I wish I could say the lesson stuck and I never used my color and nationality as an excuse to be rude again. Unfortunately, I am a slow learner. But this began a lasting journey to greater self-awareness. For that day, I realized that in rudely sticking out my tongue, I behaved in a way that I wouldn't have if the kids had been white. And I have realized as I've grown older the privilege that I have, not for any merit other than my skin color; my life has advantages that I did not earn, simply because I am white.

As an adult, I look back on that incident grateful for parents who saw my actions for what they were, rude, unacceptable behavior that had to stop.

When parents choose to raise their kids in countries where they are guests they face unique challenges. One of these is teaching children how to interact with the host country, her people, her land, her food. One of the ways to do this is through modeling, the other is through calling out bad behavior for what it is, allowing no excuses, no buts, no second chances. Because Love is not rude.

Cultural Humility

As soon as the angry words came out of my mouth, I regretted them. I was speaking to Rehmet, the woman who helped me care for my kids and my home.

Rehmet was Punjabi. She was uneducated, illiterate, with a smile that stretched across a beautiful, weathered face and a personality as big as her smile. We were living in Islamabad, and Rehmet had come into my life by way of her husband who had done some handiwork for us around the house. She had five children and lived in a slum on the outskirts of the city. She worked and talked tirelessly. At one point, I despaired to my mom that I couldn't understand her. "She speaks so quickly!" I wailed. "My Urdu can't keep up." My mom began to laugh. "Don't worry" she said. "She's actually speaking Punjabi."

We had slowly developed a relationship that went far beyond employee/employer. She was my friend. We would sit down with tea, communicating with my limited Urdu and her fluent Punjabi. We would mate socks together, cook, scrub vegetables, and rearrange furniture. She loved my kids, and I thought I loved her. But there we were. A Pakistani woman and an American woman side by side, as I let my tongue loose. She had ruined some clothes by bleaching them and I was angry. If this had happened in the United States I would voice disapproval over the mistake and demand my money back.

But, I was not in the United States. Looking back on the event, I cringe in embarrassment. I don't even remember what the clothes looked like — but I will never forget the sadness and resignation on Rehmet's face. She looked as though she had been kissed by a Judas, betrayed by one she thought she knew.

I began to apologize. My speech, so articulate while angry, suddenly lost any semblance of coherence. I fumbled with my words, with my grammar, most of all over my ugly heart. She looked at me with tired, brown eyes, her gaze steady and unyielding. Then without pause, she shrugged and said, "It doesn't matter. This is my fate."

I went cold. I would rather have heard anything but this. I would rather she yelled, screamed, got sarcastic, quit the job. Anything would have been better. I, the person who talked long and wrote hard about wanting to empower people, had taken advantage of what I knew to be a cultural value, a servant is subservient to the employer. In a culture where she was a minority — a woman, a Christian — she would never have other opportunities. This was her fate. Even if she wanted to walk out on the job, she couldn't. Rehmet did not have choices, and I had used that against her. I had taken advantage of education, relative wealth, and influence in my ridiculous reaction to a simple mistake.

And I had done this, subconsciously knowing that it would pack a mighty punch. That is what made it so painfully wrong. My white-skinned entitlement made me cringe. Who was I? Why had I reacted this way? It was important to confess — to

Rehmet, but also to God. For I had acted in a way that hurt another, had wounded knowing she had no recourse.

Rehmet and I were able to repair the relationship, largely because of her generosity of spirit and sheer joy in life. In her bucket of life experience, this was small change and she would not remain low for long. But the story has stayed with me, for it reminds me of the importance of cultural humility.

Cultural humility demands self-evaluation and critique, constant effort to understand the view of another before we react. It requires that we recognize our own tendency toward cultural superiority. Cultural humility gives up the role of expert, instead seeing ourselves as students of our host culture. It puts us on our knees, the best posture possible for learning.

Goodbyes

No matter where these goodbyes have taken place, whether it's been on hot tarmacs, or dusty river banks; efficient European airports or train stations, the symptoms are the same. My stomach gets those characteristic 'goodbye' butterflies, my throat constricts, my body feels restless. Time passes too quickly; minutes count, hours horrify.

I Didn't Look Back

I was in London's Heathrow Airport, crowds of people going to and fro. Some went quickly, late for connections and needing to get to their gate as soon as possible. Others, with hours to wait before their connections to places across the world, were walking slowly, herding children overwhelmed with baggage.

I was eighteen years old and had just graduated from high school in Pakistan. I had left all I knew and was, for the first time, heading into a world where I would not have my parents or small community to support me. I would be alone.

My parents and younger brother were with me. We had stayed in London for a couple of days of sightseeing and fun, and now I was heading off to Scotland to visit my best friend and a favorite teacher alone. I would first go to Glasgow and then catch a train up to Fraserburgh in Aberdeenshire, Scotland, where the summer daylight lasts until late night and fishing is the primary occupation.

I remember hugging my parents and brother and heading off with my suitcase, passport, and ticket in hand.

They remember that I didn't look back.

I didn't look back. Like Lot's wife in the well-known Biblical story, I was afraid if I looked back I would turn to salt, an immobile statue. I would be unable to move from that point. These changes were big changes. And if I looked back — I wouldn't have been able to move forward.

Although it had points of deep pain and longing, boarding school angst and misunderstanding, my childhood was all that I had. And I loved it. It was the only thing that anchored me to community. Pakistan and the small communities of missionaries and Pakistanis who made up my world — that was all that I knew. Oh I knew travel, I knew passports, tickets, airports, trains, negotiating life in a place far from my passport country. But Pakistan was home. It was where my heart was understood. How could I leave it?

I knew intuitively that if I looked back then all of that would flood over me and it would be over before it began.

And so — I didn't look back. I couldn't look back.

The Bittersweet Taste of Goodbye

We are up early. While the rest of the house is sleeping, our college-bound girl is doing her last-minute packing, grabbing a winter coat she forgot in the eighty-nine degrees and ninety percent humidity of our August morning, trying to calm her stomach. And I begin to reflect on that bittersweet word "Goodbye."

Third culture kids and international travelers know these words well. At six years old I was driven, with my older brothers, to the Hyderabad train station to catch a train that would take me eight hundred miles to Rawalpindi. There a large army-green bus would take us the remaining two hours to our boarding school in the hill station of Murree. On the train station platform my tears flowed without embarrassment. I was only six. And even after all these years, the bitter taste of goodbye and all that meant for me is a sweet and hard memory. For my mother the hardest part came after the train rolled away, when tears stopped and hers fell. When she arrived home, she found my favorite doll. In the midst of the goodbye chaos, I had left her at home. But I was with friends. As soon as the train left the station, my world was immersed in six-year-old imagination and friendship.

That was the first of more goodbyes than I could possibly count. Whoever first coined the adjective "bittersweet" had tremendous insight. For when we say goodbye we usually know that what is beyond will be wonderful for the person to who is leaving. But the present brings up that familiar knot in the stomach, a mixture of pain, sadness, and nervousness.

What I remember more than goodbye is waking up the first morning in an unfamiliar bed and in complete confusion until I remembered that this was boarding. I had left home. Mom was not there. But the hot tears that fell on my six-year-old face were accompanied by that clear whisper, the voice of God himself. "I am with you." Those are the words I still hope each of my children hear as they say their frequent goodbyes.

Goodbye – God Be With You

We arrived at JFK airport and headed to the line that bore the banner "U.S. Citizens." The majority of the passengers on the plane headed to one of two other lines, Residents or Visitors, located farther along in the large impersonal immigration area.

We said goodbye the evening before to my daughter, Annie, and to my eldest son, Joel. Joel was staying on with Annie in Cairo for two weeks. We held each other tightly and did not want to let go. We wished that we lived closer. Just as my mom would love to pop over for a cup of tea to my house without planning, so would I have loved to grab tea or coffee with my oldest daughter spontaneously, without purchasing a plane ticket. Through many years and many goodbyes I somehow, mysteriously missed the origin of the word "goodbye." When I learned that goodbye comes from "God be with you" the word changed completely for me. To say "God be with you" is at the heart of my world. To say "Goodbye" to my kids with that meaning in mind is a comfort to my 'mom' heart.

The goodbyes represented in the JFK immigration area were many. We were all strangers to each other, so who knows the scope of the stories and goodbyes that were there. But knowing many immigrants, all with amazing and poignant life stories, allowed me to understand how much lies beneath that which is visible, how much is under the surface. Some of us were permanent residents of the U.S., probably visiting relatives in Cairo, now back home. Others were newcomers to the U.S., looking slightly confused, making their way to the wrong lines, revealing their unfamiliarity with the rules.

Those of you who are reading this book are no stranger to goodbyes. Perhaps your first goodbyes were at age of six or seven as you went to boarding school for the first time, brave on the surface, stomach knotting inside as you passed through that boarding school "rite of passage" for the first time. Others may have said your first goodbyes in high school, going back to your passport country to complete school. For others it was when you got married and left your family home, entering into a new world with your in-laws or a world apart with your new husband, so young he could hardly grow a beard.

Regardless of when it was, the feelings of nervous stomach and throat catching are universal. Butterflies and uneasy energy seem to take over. Tears remain unshed, stored up for a more private time to be shed like water on a parched land. All the world feels caught in these goodbyes, goodbyes that bruise and hurt, yet remind us that our hearts are still soft and alive. For a dead heart doesn't hurt with a goodbye, only a heart alive to others feels the pain of that goodbye, the difficulty of leaving.

May I forever hurt with the goodbyes that I say. May I forever remember the strength of the words "God Be With You."

202

Negotiating Reentry

I don't know why I started arguing with airport security. It was stupid and irrational. But I wasn't in a space to be rational. I had just traveled thirty-six hours from Karachi and had landed at JFK. The warmth and developing world chaos of Karachi contrasted with New York's crowds and control. It was an icy reentry into an already cold season. I was once again the square peg in a round hole.

I somehow made it through the nasty interaction that followed and sank into my airport chair, my face burning with embarrassment, chagrin, and pure pain. I didn't belong in this world. I knew it with every fiber of who I was. But this was my legal address, and for now I needed to accept that.

I've done a lot of reentering. Reentry is returning, after an extensive time away from your passport country, to the world where your legal address is housed. Reentry is tricky. It's uncomfortable and scratchy. It wears like an ill-fitting coat, enveloping and smothering what's inside. It comes with loneliness and can breed nasty bouts of self-pity. And the discomfort is usually in proportion to how long you've been away. It's one thing to go on a semester abroad; it's entirely another to reenter after fifteen years. While the reentry difficulties a college student feels are valid, reentry after a long period is far more pronounced.

The concept of reentry has roots in the criminal justice system. Criminal offenders who had been in the prison system needed help to transition back to life outside the system, to 'normal' life. A study done in the U.S in 2006 found that two-thirds of offenders released from the system would be rearrested within three years time. Reentry programs are designed to break the cycle of release and re-incarceration with the hope of healthy and permanent transition into society. Effective reentry programs help the person develop the life skills necessary to become healthy, productive members of society.

Reentry for the expat and global nomad is a bit different. We feel like outsiders, foreigners, in places where we are supposed to belong. While we were away the lens through which we view the world has changed, the world we left has changed, even if it's initially not apparent, and we have changed. Just like a new pair of glasses has us tripping and spinning, so does reentry.

Disorientation, confusion, frustration, and anxiety are a few of the feelings that can arise while negotiating reentry. While there are profound differences between reentry as defined by the criminal justice system and reentry as defined by the expat or global nomad, the end goal is similar, a healthy transition into society. But what is healthy transition into society? And how do we do it when our world is spinning and our hearts feel exiled?

The standard response to that question is to talk about stages of reentry. Indeed there are stages. Stage one, often called disengagement, begins before we've left. This is where we go through the tasks, both physical and emotional, of leaving, packing up, and saying goodbye. Stage two, euphoria, puts us in a honeymoon stage, a time where we're excited to be with family whom we've missed, eat foods that we've fantasized about, and do things that we couldn't while away. This is a remarkable time. Stage three, alienation, takes us where we don't want to go, to reverse culture shock, dislike of what we see in our passport country, anger at the 'norms' that we never thought about before we left, frustration at our families and friends for not getting it. And then we come to stage four, gradual readjustment, a stage where we integrate back into a new normal, taking that which we've learned and making it a part of us, even as we accept that we have returned.

If we were robots, these stages would make perfect sense. They would flow one into the other on a smooth trajectory. We would look in the mirror and say "Don't worry, you're just in stage three. Soon everything will be better." But we're not robots, and this is anything but a smooth process. So beyond the stages of reentry, what do we need to reenter?

We need to leave at peace with our colleagues, our friends, our church, our community, and our adopted homeland. Sure, there were hard things, but if we leave at peace, we can start in peace. This is huge and I've never heard anyone stress how important it is.

We must recognize that there is no way we can do this alone. Just as a recovering addict recognizes his or her need for a 'higher power,' so it is with us. We need help. Whether that be a friend or counselor, it's too hard to do it alone. Yes,

God is there and he is ever-present; sometimes it helps when he has skin on.

We need to find ways to tell our stories. This may be to a person, or it may be in a journal. Whatever the medium, we must tell the story. It is uniquely ours, it is critical to who we have become. This was one of the reasons I began writing. I had to have an outlet for my stories, for things I saw, felt, heard. We must tell our story and tell it loud.

We must eat well and exercise. This is critical, but I rarely hear it addressed. Weight gain, in my case, a lot of weight gain is a serious danger. The food is completely different. We sometimes joked that one piece of chicken in the United States would serve our whole family. A change in diet is an emotional roller coaster. Not only do we feel at odds with our surroundings, we're at odds with our bodies as well. Eating a healthy diet, making sure we have protein and Vitamin C (our healers), and coupling it with exercise, even if it's minimal, can get our bodies out of the reentry slump. Exercise brings out our endorphins and we will physically feel more able, and stronger.

If possible, we need to find a restaurant that serves the food we've left behind in our adopted country. While it seems really simple, the familiarity of smells and tastes can kill the *saudade*, if only for a while. If you can't find a restaurant in your area, set aside one day of the week to cook foods from your adopted country. Your whole family is at different stages of adjustment to their new surroundings, so it will benefit all of you. Use it as a time to reminisce, then move forward.

We should use precious items from the places we love, but have left, to decorate our homes. Don't buy in to the latest and greatest from glossy home décor magazines! You have Unique, You have Amazing, You have Beautiful. Meld it into your style and display things that are beloved and familiar.

We must learn to grieve well. Grieving is something that we often don't allow ourselves to do. Yet grieving is crucial to being able to move on. To name our losses, to grieve them, allows us to move forward in a more realistic and healthy way.

We must pick our safe people. Not everyone is safe. Pray for discernment that you will know who to share with and who not to. I've made the mistake of assuming all will get it. There are those who, despite good intentions, will make you feel worse. These are the 'Pull up your bootstraps and get on with it' folks. While there is a time when putting on boots, and pulling up those clichéd bootstraps is necessary, there's also a time when you have no boots on. First you have to get the boots. Only then can you use them effectively. We are created for community, created to 'belong.' And some of our struggles with reentry are feeling that our place is taken away. Finding safe people is a step towards 'belonging.' We may still feel like our outside world is alien, but inside with that safe friend, drinking tea, crying, laughing, and getting powdered sugar on our upper lips from pastries, we belong.

Negotiating reentry can be as simple as a few weeks and as complicated as seven years. Know that others are in this journey with you and for you.

Thoughts on Entry from a Third Culture Kid

When I began looking into information on refugee resettlement and orientation programs for refugees entering a country, I was struck by how much the advice resonated with me as a third culture kid. The TCK experience and the refugee experience are worlds apart. But the goals and the realistic expectations developed for refugee orientation programs are remarkably helpful.

Orientation for the refugee is not just about theory and information, it is also designed to give the refugee "the opportunity to develop realistic expectations regarding their resettlement, to consider different situations that might arise in a new country, and develop skills and attitudes that will facilitate their adjustment and well being." Here are my TCK reentry resettlement and orientation recommendations:

Form realistic time expectations. Entering a new world is a journey. It doesn't happen in three months or six months. Think about how long our parents took to adjust to their adopted country. Give yourself a minimum of two years, but don't be surprised if it takes five. This is a new world we're in and it deserves all the attention we would give to going into a totally different culture. So you spent summers here every once in a while when you were a kid? Transitioning to our passport country is bigger than spending a summer vacation.

Accept that we are a combination of worlds. As TCKs our worlds are woven together in a semi-formed tapestry. Many of us feel like completely different people when we're in our passport countries. This doesn't mean we're schizophrenic. It means we're juggling roles, we're weighing what is appropriate to say and who is safe. We are not chameleons and we are not impostors. Rather we are trying to make sense of our worlds and figure out what cultural adaptation looks like as we effectively transition to our passport countries. Yes, there is loss of identity. But as we work through these losses, our identities, as those who can live between worlds, emerge stronger than ever.

Understand culture shock. Culture shock in degrees is inevitable. And it often takes a while to surface. We don't go through reverse culture shock. We just go through culture shock. Reverse culture shock means we know a culture, have been away from it, and are returning to differences we didn't expect. In our case, we don't really know this culture we are entering. We may think we know it, because our passports tell us we should, but we don't. Not really. And while reverse culture shock is described as "wearing contact lenses in the wrong eyes," culture shock is having completely different lenses.

Give voice to a longing. Struggling to give voice to our longings is enormously important. Somehow it doesn't feel valid. But giving voice to our longings is legitimate. Our world, as we know it, has come to an end. We may be able to visit our home, our adopted country, but we know that we must have a valid and legal way to stay there should we wish to go back. We will have times of intense longing and wistfulness for what no longer exists. Giving voice to this longing, this *saudade*, helps take away its power and ability to control. The longings are there, they are valid, but if they control us we will despair. Our longings can be expressed through writing, through connecting to other TCKs, through the visual arts, through theatre, through faith, and through friendships, but they must be expressed.

Understand the shaping of our worldview. While our parents went overseas with already developed worldviews, and through their interactions in their host countries had their worldviews challenged and changed, our worldview was formed in our host country. Our first memories are rarely of our passport country. Rather they are of our host country. If your ideas and conception of the world began with memories of the call to prayer, or a dusty road and traffic jam involving a buffalo, two donkey carts, and your parent's jeep, or a crowded and colorful bazaar filled with colorful fabrics and bangles, then it's highly unlikely you'll be suspicious of Muslims, or that you will hate crowds, or that you will be scared of traffic jams. Our perceptions are shaped from early on, and our perceptions differ markedly from those of our parents, those of our peers in our passport countries, and those in our churches. Having realistic expectations on differing worldviews helps us to not expect or demand that others understand.

Accept that faith can be complicated. For many of us, faith is paramount to who we are. But it gets tangled up in our adjusting to life in our passport countries. It's particularly difficult if we feel we can't question God, express disbelief or doubt, or change denominations because it feels disloyal to our parents. If we have good relationships with our parents we care about what they think. This can inhibit our honesty as it relates to our faith journeys. If we're struggling with identity and belonging in college and get a call from our parents that inevitably ends up with "Are you going to church and getting connected?" we can feel worse. How do we tell them "No. I can't stand church." "Are you praying about this?" they say with love in their voices and tears in their eyes, and we want to say "Maybe the question is 'am I praying at all?'" They're miles away and desperate to know we are okay. Perhaps doubts were never a part of our faith journey before, but now that the world around us has become unfamiliar, the doubts surface. Who is this God I thought I trusted? Does he care? Will the faith that sustained us through my journey thus far be big enough to get me through this crucial juncture? Those are important questions, valid questions, and sometimes our parents handle them well. Other times, we may need to find those others who can hear them, understand them, and speak truth into them.

Value cultural brokers. Often there emerges that key person, the person who doesn't share our background but understands in a way that defies our understanding. This is a gift. This is the person who explains life to us, who walks beside us. This is the one who looks through our high school yearbook and says "Now who's this with you? And did you go on that camping trip where you got in trouble for sneaking over to where the boys were sleeping before or after this picture was taken?" This personal interest helps us understand what friendship, listening, and cultural brokering look like. Learn from them. Look to them. But don't put undue burdens on them.

Acknowledge place and its significance. At our core, as humans, is a need for 'place.' Call it 'belonging,' call it 'home,' call it anything you like. But all of us are integrally connected to place. We are "incarnate beings" and so when those places are taken away, we suffer from a "disruption" of place. It is clear that the TCK has a disruption of place – and often multiple times in their lives. If the disruption goes beyond our ability to adapt it becomes a pathology – the late Paul Tournier, a gifted Swiss psychologist, calls this a "deprivation of place." He says that to be human is to need a place, to be rooted and attached to that place. Many of us downplay this connection to place by over spiritualizing it or underestimating its importance, but I have come to an absolute conviction that God uses place. He uses place from the minute we are born to the day of our last breath. He brought Abraham out of Ur. He took Joseph to Egypt. He brought Ruth to Israel. They were all expatriates or third culture kids and God used place to work out the details of their lives. In God we are given a full allowance and understanding of this need. We need not dismiss it, we need not idolize it; we can acknowledge it and recognize it as valid.

Allow our hearts to yearn. All of us have a heart that yearns for belonging, for acceptance, for love. This is the human condition. It's a fundamental truth and it is not unique to the third culture kid. What is hard is tying this in with all of our TCK experiences, life story, and worldview. It is easy for us to think that we yearn only for that which we left. In reality, we had hearts that yearned before we ever left our passport countries. If we can grow in an understanding of our hearts, what is global and universal in our yearning, and what is specifically tied to being a third culture kid, we are in a good place. A desire for place is universal, a desire for our particular place, whether Buenos Aires or Bolivia or Cairo or Lebanon, is specific to our TCK background.

Accept and offer grace. It is so easy to want grace, and so hard to give grace. Yet all of this is about grace, the grace that we were given by our host country, the grace of others who walked beside us as kids, the grace of our parents in caring and loving even when they don't fully understand. Most of all, the grace of God. Those of us who 'get' grace will find it easier to give grace. Indeed this is my daily prayer — that I will never forget the grace I've been shown and that this will shape my responses by the day, the hour, and the minute. The big questions are these: Can we give grace to those who dismiss us, hurt us, misunderstand us, or don't like us? Can we give grace to the people whom we misunderstand, whom we don't like, whom we dismiss?

There is so much more that I think and feel. More too that I've not thought about. Although there are similarities that bind us together as TCK's, ultimately we each have our own unique story. I may have walked a similar path, but you own your story. None of this is a formula, it's not a list of stages, but it is my earned fact, and that is perhaps more valuable.

To the Displaced and the Exile

I get it. You sit in a crowd of people, and you feel your mouth go dry. The bite you just took from your scone chokes in your throat. How can you be this lonely in a crowd? How is it possible that your passport country feels so alien?

You were excited to return. There were many things you were sick of in your adopted country. You were tired of the dirt. You had had enough of the chaos. You had to boil water one time too many, and you forgot to soak the vegetables in iodine solution. Your visiting guest came down with dysentery. Your household help, whom you love, complained and asked for more money, and you simultaneously felt angry and guilty. You have so much. She has so little. But it is not that simple.

You felt alien in your other world. The last few weeks were chaotic and hot. There were so many people to see, so many projects to finish, children to prepare, suitcases to pack. You read an article on burnout and knew that was you. You could hardly wait to go to a coffee shop and order coffee in your own language, not tripping over verbs and adjectives.

But as you look around, you let out a soul-deep sigh. You pictured all this so differently. You thought it would be so good, such a rest, such a time of peace. But you had barely arrived when you realized that life had moved on here. You call your best friend. She squeals with delight and then says "I'm so sorry. Can't talk now! Heading to a work party. Gotta get the kids ready for the baby sitter. And next week we're swamped! Kids are getting ready for camp. We've got church stuff. Can't wait to catch up."

Oh. And your siblings. Oh. Your. Siblings. You so want to be able to sit down with them, to share life. But two of your brother's have wives that are not speaking to each other and the idea of a fun family dinner is just that, an idea. So there you sit. All of this going through your mind. And you feel one hot tear trickle down your face. You brush it away impatiently. But there's another. How can you escape and just let all the preceding weeks and the now fill up your tear ducts and fall freely, a red sniffly nose and all?

You are displaced. You feel you are in exile. You've no home to go to. You're not fully at home there, but neither are you here. You make it to the car and sit. It's begun to rain and the rain blocks the windows, sending streams of water down and hiding you from the world. It has been a long time since you've seen rain. Your tears fall like the heavy raindrops. You sob like you will never stop. There is no one to hold you. There is no one to offer tangible, concrete comfort.

Slowly the sobs swallow you up. You begin to feel such relief, the relief that comes only from a cry so deep you can't explain it.

And somehow you know that God is there. The God you cried to for weeks before making the move, late at night when all were sleeping so as to upset no one. The God who was with you when you held your two-year-old in a steamy bathroom, far from good medical care, praying that the croup would go. The God who was with you when you first arrived on the soil of another country, looking out-of-place and oh so tired. The God who you prayed to when you went off the road in a car accident in the middle of nowhere and suddenly help was available.

The God of the Displaced and the Exiled is with you. Here and Now. You recall the verse given to you by an older woman who knew what this nomadic life would hold, who knew the good and the hard. You breathe. Slowly.

You say the verse aloud, your voice raspy, knowing you are at the end of your human strength. "Blessed are those whose strength is in you; whose hearts are set on pilgrimage. As they pass through the Valley of Baka, they make it a place of springs; the autumn rains also cover it with pools. They go from strength to strength, until each appears before God in Zion."

Softly you repeat the words "Strength to strength" and you start the car.

The Moving Manifesto

Be ruthless. Don't go into memory mode. Keep telling yourself "I don't need to feel that attached to it." Bite back your tears. Remind yourself that your life is exciting, that others should be as lucky as you. Try not to listen when friends begin talking about an event that is coming in the future, after you're gone. Tell your kids numerous times that they will get to have a 'new room' and 'new friends' where you are going. Repeat "Isn't that so exciting?" often.

This is the Moving Manifesto. As days fill with parties and packing, numerous goodbyes, short tempers, unexpected tears in public and private places, we who have traveled this road many times must remember this manifesto. We are comrades of sorts, traveling a path not everybody travels, loyal to each other and to change, unable to explain to people that though we cry now, we really would not trade our lives. But we need to express those deep feelings of loss and grief in order to do what we do, and do it well.

We go into auto-mode once it becomes inevitable that the packing must be done. Until then, a part of us pretends life will always be as it is right now. Occasionally we purchase items for our current reality, almost as a talisman against what's coming, or a nesting despite knowing that very soon the nest will be knocked from the tree and it will take a while to rebuild. We are well aware that some of our current relationships will survive the move, and others will not. Not everybody has the capacity to maintain friendships that withstand distance and change. We will not hold that against them. But we are allowed to feel sad. That is part of the manifesto.

And all too soon, that final party will come. We will be the life of that party. We will retell stories with our old friends. We won't admit to ourselves that they were not part of our lives three, four, or five years before, because that would give in to the idea that it's ok that we are moving, and right now it's not ok.

As the day arrives, the manifesto becomes more important. Part of this process is frustration with our current situation. If we can be mad at 'right now' our future looks much easier and brighter. Everything that can possibly go wrong often does just that. The moving truck doesn't have a permit, the moving people break your favorite clock, your best friend has an emergency and is not there to help, your other friends show up like Job's friends, telling you everything you are doing wrong. And your kids? They realize this is a reality, suddenly recognize they are displaced people, and the tears are unstoppable. Hours later, final goodbyes are said with a sinking feeling, and a catch in the voice. As you drive away, you do not look back. For perhaps you will, like Lot's wife in the Biblical account, turn to stone.

Yet you survive. Two days and hours of jet lag later, you are in your new location, figuring out how to make it a home.

It all feels like a dream. Neighbors have looked curiously at your family, trying to assess your kids' ages. One conversation has already felt promising. It is time for a different manifesto.

The Arrival Manifesto

In the past week, the sidewalks of Boston have been covered with boxes, suitcases, garment bags, trunks, and the occasional stuffed animal, a remnant from childhoods that went by too quickly. Massive laundry baskets are lined up to take all the earthly goods that a college student was allowed to take from home, to rooms that are around 6 feet wide, 10 feet long, and badly in need of remodeling.

The Moving Manifesto was born out of the millions of memories I have of packing up houses and leaving places from as far as Pakistan to as close as Cambridge. As I hear from one of my children, a freshman in college, and observe neighbors and students in our area, I realize that as difficult as the moving manifesto is, the arrival manifesto can be just as painful.

Here is my arrival manifesto for settling and surviving:

Force conversation. Don't give too much information, they might think you're boasting. Keep on telling yourself "In a couple of weeks this will all seem familiar." Bite back your tears. Remind yourself that you always made friends before. Surely you can make friends now. Force yourself to not look at Facebook to see what all your friends back home are doing. If you cannot stay away from Facebook, post pictures that make it look like you are having the time of your life with your new" friends (who are not really your friends yet, but who's to know?) Quickly scout out your surroundings and find a coffee place that you think could become a favorite. Don't call your mom, because she'll stay up all night in tears thinking you are not ever going to be ok and wondering how her baby girl or boy will survive without her. No, this last one you won't be able to do.

Settling and surviving is hard work. I am convinced that it is made more difficult by our ability to monitor our old life through the click of a mouse. In just one click you can see the party that you couldn't go to because you've moved. One click will show you that the critical part you played in your school or community is now being played by someone else, and brings on a wave of inadequacy and the sense that you are easily replaced. Added to that are the high expectations that we place on ourselves, feeling like it shouldn't take so long to adjust, as if we are doing something wrong because we don't feel fully connected and everyone else seems to be doing so well.

Identity crises are frequent in the first days of a move. Going from places where we are known, where our skills and talents are recognized and appreciated, to a place where no one knows anything about us can be simultaneously freeing and terrifying. Having to explain everything about our families, our manners and our quirks with the potential for misunderstanding is a vulnerable place to be.

Yet moving is worth it. It's not easy, it never will be. It brings out the best and worst of me, often at the same time, and it can be an assault on my security. Despite all that, I can't imagine the opportunities I would have missed and the people I would never have met had I not been willing to go through the settling process and move into surviving and thriving.

So if you are one of those that just made a move, or remember with pain a recent move where you still aren't sure where and how you fit, think of it like a pair of new shoes. You saw them in the store and they looked so cute. You tried them on and they fit! They looked great. Then you took them home. You put them on again. You didn't remember that they were that tight, or that you couldn't walk in them that well. You try wearing the shoes for a while, but a tiny blister forms making it even more difficult to walk. So you take them off, wondering why you liked them in the first place. But the next day you try again because you do like them and you paid good money for them, and you'll try again the day after. You do this and wear them a bit longer.

Day after day you break those shoes in, getting compliments because they are cute, and you look good in them. Then suddenly you wake up one day, you go to put them on and you realize they no longer hurt. They feel great. In fact, they've become your favorite pair of shoes. Part of the moving manifesto is that this move, like the shoes, could become your favorite.

Reunions

For the third culture kid reunions are many and frequent. Hellos are also frequent, goodbyes more so. Trying to work through the complexity of being willing to get to know someone only to let them go is a challenge. We often feel it's not worthwhile, that the goodbyes are too painful. Dave Pollock who worked extensively with third culture kids until his death tells us that unresolved grief will be a major struggle for us:

> One of the major areas in working with TCKs is that of...dealing with the issue of unresolved grief. They are always leaving or being left. Relationships are short-lived. At the end of each school year, a certain number of the student body leaves, not just for the summer, but for good. It has to be up to the parent to provide a framework of support and careful understanding as the child learns to deal with this repetitive grief. Most TCKs go through more grief experiences by the time they are twenty than monocultural individuals do in a lifetime.

This cycle of goodbyes and unresolved grief is also self-perpetuating. Just as we said many goodbyes and faced continuous loss as kids, we bring up our children with a love of travel and the world so we continue to face these partings. Only now it's with our most precious asset, our kids.

Then we go through that glorious feeling of reunion. We hug so tightly we can hardly breathe and we can't talk fast enough to get all the missing thoughts and words of the last months and years out of our hearts and heads and into the hearts and heads of the other person. In that instant, no matter how much it hurts to say goodbye, the reunion is all the sweeter. As much as we think we want that other person's life, the life of the one who has lived in the same house for thirty years and has all of their family within a five mile radius, it will never be so for us. And during the sweet space of reunion we can say that's quite alright !

Rearranging Furniture, Crossing Borders

It's that time again. No matter how adjusted I become, restlessness is in my bones, born out of years of living between worlds, three months at a time in boarding, three more months at home, back to boarding, on to summer housing in Murree, and every fourth year to my passport country. These frequent moves produced a need to either wander or rearrange furniture. Sometimes both. It's a restlessness that cannot be tamed. My mother recently told me that she realized once my brothers and I turned six years old we never slept in the same bed for more than three months at a time until adulthood. I come by this honestly.

My two 'best practices' in dealing with the restless wandering are to rearrange the furniture or head to the closest international border. For a long time I thought that everybody liked to rearrange furniture and travel. But it's not so. Many people love the comfort of familiarity, predictable people and predictable furniture. Then there are those of us who feel almost a physical discomfort when things are too static and change too slow. It creeps over us like a rash, healed only by the scrape of a couch across a floor, or a customs officer asking us if we have "anything to declare."

Communicating this restlessness is a challenge. It often comes across as discontent, and we are told to "Pull up our bootstraps and get on with it." But when you are hardwired to this nomadic life, pulling up your bootstraps has nothing to do with it. A year after moving from Cairo to the U.S., my husband, a military kid and familiar with change, saw the restlessness come over me in a wave manifesting itself in tears and "everybody in America hates me."

"Pack your bags, kids!" he said. "We're going to Quebec City!" and we did. Just like that. Four hours away and my entire outlook had changed. We had crossed over a border and were ordering savory crepes, in French, at a café. It was only a three-day trip over a holiday weekend, but it was enough to pacify the wandering restlessness. Until the next time. The next time I rearranged the furniture. It was cheaper.

In the developing world, adventures and stories of the unimaginable are a part of daily life. Who has their appendix taken out by a CIA agent? Only a third culture kid. In the more predictable West, adventures aren't as frequent and sometimes have to be made. Rearranging furniture or planning a trip are symbolic to me of creating adventure when adventure seems slow in coming.

So it's that time of year. Time to rearrange the furniture, or leave for the International Terminal, passport in hand and board a non-stop flight time to journey across oceans to visit friends or relatives or simply go somewhere that feels like home. It's my antidote to that restless wandering, and part of my adjustment comes in realizing that it's ok. I am wired this way. There will come a day when the trips will either not exist, or I will be too old to travel. When that day comes, I'll rearrange my dresser and have my stories, stories of the unimaginable sort that my grandchildren will think I fabricated.

I Don't Do Goodbye

Recently, we said goodbye to my younger brother and his wife beside a ferryboat in Istanbul. In the grand scheme of goodbyes, this was surely not the hardest, but it still stung. Making it more difficult, another brother and his wife arrived from Kazakhstan and Cyprus and we had an unexpected family reunion. We collectively decided Turkey is an excellent place for a family reunion.

We arrived on a grey, chilly Saturday afternoon and drank *sahlep* on the banks of the Bosphorous before catching a ferry to the Asian side of Istanbul. Our first meal held the magic of a crowded shopping area, a soccer game between warring teams viewed on a television perched high above the crowd, and kebabs that filled the mouth with tastes of the Middle East. Every day was filled with belonging and connection. And then it was over. We had to say goodbye.

For the one whose heart is set on pilgrimage, goodbyes add up. It's not the arithmetic that brings the sting. That can be shared through guessing games and laughter at dinner with friends. "Let's have a contest! How many places have you lived in? How many goodbyes have you said? How many airports have you traveled through?" No, it's not in the math. It is what's behind the math: the faces, the events, the places, the people, the tight chest, the throat constricting.

Goodbyes hurt.

Since the first goodbye when I left for Murree for the first time, I have said hundreds of goodbyes. No matter where these goodbyes have taken place, whether it's been on hot tarmacs, or dusty riverbanks, efficient European airports or train stations, the symptoms are the same. My stomach gets those characteristic 'goodbye' butterflies, my throat constricts, my body feels restless. Time passes too quickly, minutes count, hours horrify.

I asked my family to help me write about "Saying goodbye." I needed input that would satisfy those of us who have collectively said more goodbyes than can be counted. While their advice was of minimal help, the request made us all laugh and that helped tremendously.

It was my sister-in-law, a woman who grew up in Kenya, lived in Massachusetts, Turkey, Kazakhstan, and most recently Denver, and has said hundreds of goodbyes, who captured the moment.

"I don't do 'good-bye'!" she said. "But I love you."

And that is how we said goodbye.

EGYPT مصر

٨٣٢ دسن

CPSIA information can be obtained at www.ICGtesting.com
Printed in the USA
LVOW13s0806200714

395089LV00005B/438/P